ROCKHOUNDING
Pennsylvania
and New Jersey

A Guide to the States' Best Rockhounding Sites

ROBERT D. BEARD

FALCONGUIDES

GUILFORD, CONNECTICUT
HELENA, MONTANA
AN IMPRINT OF GLOBE PEQUOT PRESS

FALCON GUIDES®

Copyright © 2013 Morris Book Publishing, LLC

FalconGuides is an imprint of Globe Pequot Press.
Falcon, FalconGuides, and Outfit Your Mind are registered trademarks of Morris Book Publishing, LLC.

Maps by Daniel Lloyd © Morris Book Publishing, LLC
Project editor: Meredith Dias
Text design: Sheryl P. Kober
Layout: Sue Murray

Library of Congress Cataloging-in-Publication Data

Beard, Robert D.
 Rockhounding Pennsylvania and New Jersey : a guide to the states' best rockhounding sites / Robert D. Beard.
  p. cm.
 Includes bibliographical references and index.
 ISBN 978-0-7627-8093-8
 1. Rocks—Collection and preservation—Pennsylvania—Guidebooks. 2. Rocks—Collection and preservation—New Jersey—Guidebooks. 3. Minerals—Collection and preservation—Pennsylvania—Guidebooks. 4. Minerals—Collection and preservation—New Jersey—Guidebooks. 5. Pennsylvania—Guidebooks. 6. New Jersey—Guidebooks. I. Title.
 QE445.P46B43 2013
 557.48—dc23
                                                                                    2012033953
Printed in the United States of America

CONTENTS

Ridge and Valley Province

Appalachian Plateaus Province

New Jersey Sites
Coastal Plain Province

Piedmont Province

Highlands Province

Pennsylvania

Lake Erie

OHIO

NEW YORK

WEST VIRGINIA

MARYLAND

DE.

NEW JERSEY

APPALACHIAN PLATEAU

RIDGE AND VALLEY

PIEDMONT

NEW ENGLAND

N

25 mi.

25 km.

Erie
Sharon
New Castle
Beaver Falls
Pittsburgh
Washington
Butler
Franklin
Meadville
Titusville
Warren
Bradford
Coudersport
Towanda
Milford
Scranton
Wilkes-Barre
Laporte
Williamsport
Liberty
Bellefonte
State College
Clearfield
Altoona
Johnstown
Indiana
Latrobe
Connellsville
Uniontown *Mt. Davis 3,128 ft*
Somerset
Bloomsburg
Hazleton
Jim Thorpe
Allentown
Reading
Lancaster
York
Harrisburg
Carlisle
Gettysburg
Chambersburg
Pottstown
Philadelphia
Bristol
Delaware Water Gap
Sunbury
Pottsville

New Jersey

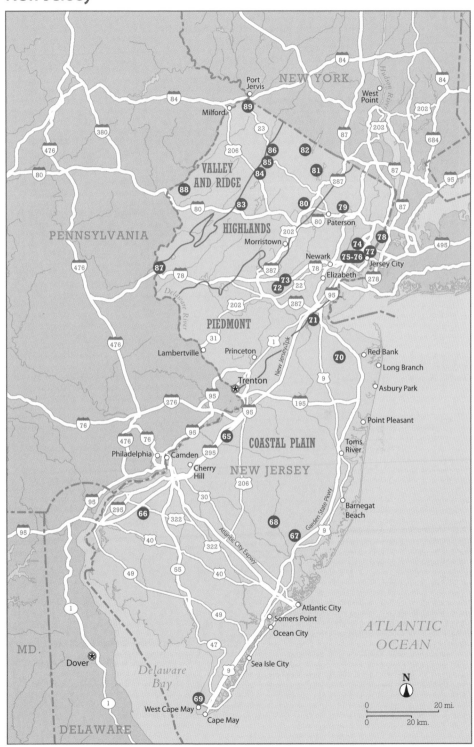

ACKNOWLEDGMENTS

This book represents more than twenty-four years of rockhounding in Pennsylvania and New Jersey, and many people have helped make this book possible. I would first like to thank my editor at *Rock & Gem* magazine, Lynn Varon, who put me in contact with Globe Pequot Press, and William Kappele, another Rockhounding series writer and contributing editor at *Rock & Gem,* who suggested me to Lynn as a potential author for this book. I would also like to thank James Miller of JMiller Media, who published my articles with *Rock & Gem* since 1993. This gave me magazine writing experience and enabled me to learn much more about rock, mineral, and fossil collecting than I ever anticipated.

I would like to thank my editors at Globe Pequot Press, Jessica Haberman and Meredith Dias, for their reviews, suggestions, and encouragement while the book was taking shape. Melissa Baker in the map department was also extremely helpful with her comments and suggestions. Many thanks are due to the production staff and the many people who were instrumental in producing and distributing the book.

I would like to thank my friends from the Central Pennsylvania Rock and Mineral Club, who always made my family and me very welcome at meetings and club field trips. In particular, I would like to thank Don and Linda Kauffman, Ed Charles, Joe Daugue, Pen Ambler, Kerry Matt, Jeri Jones, and R. J. Harris for many interesting discussions at club meetings, field trips, and especially the club's annual Gem and Mineral show. I learned a great deal about quarry collecting and many new sites from my involvement with the club. I highly recommend joining your local mineral club—all the clubs that I know in Pennsylvania and New Jersey have always welcomed new members and can teach both new and advanced collectors a great deal through their events and field trips.

Lastly, I would like to thank my family for supporting this effort, in particular my mother, Nancy Beard, and my late father, John Beard, who always encouraged my writing and came on many field trips. But most of all I would like to thank my wife, Rosalina, and our two children, Daniel and Roberta. We took many field trips together and had some very interesting adventures, particularly when getting lost in the northern New Jersey Highlands, going to iron and copper mines, and exploring the Concrete City in Pennsylvania. Rock collecting has given us many unique family adventures, and I hope that other families can share similar experiences, at least the positive ones, through the field trips in this book.

Introduction

Rock hounds encompass a very wide group, from the amateur with no background in minerals to the advanced geologist with an extensive background in mineralogy. My main objective in writing this book is to provide a reference for the fathers or mothers who want to take their kids rock collecting and need to find a place to start, and for the advanced geologist or collector who does not know Pennsylvania or New Jersey and wants to see some rocks when they visit either state. Mineral clubs, schools, and groups that want to take field trips can also use this guide, especially for sites that are conducive to larger groups. Essentially, this book is written for everyone who has an interest in minerals, rocks, and fossils and is looking for them in Pennsylvania and New Jersey.

Pennsylvania and New Jersey have a wide variety of mineral occurrences, but like much of the eastern United States, many mineral localities are on private land or public sites where mineral collecting is prohibited. In this book I have focused on identifying sites that people can visit themselves or with their families without significant advance planning or permission. Quarries and mines, although they offer great opportunities for collectors, are generally active sites and require lots of planning prior to a visit; it is often difficult for an individual, especially if you are trying to bring kids, to get into a quarry or mine on short notice.

The sites described in this book are worth a visit as long as they are accessible. It is imperative to obey all signs and obtain permission to access off-limits areas when it is required. Just because a site is described in this book does not mean it will remain accessible or that collecting is permitted on the site. I have personally checked every one of the sites in this book. Many of the sites are roadcuts, roadside "borrow pits," or outcrops that are somewhat limited in size but are reasonably accessible for visitors. Roadcuts are often within the highway right-of-way and sometimes belong to the state or local government. Generally, you can collect in these areas if they are safe and you are not disrupting traffic. In general, if an outcrop, roadcut, or pit is not posted, I have listed the site in this book but with the caveat that land and access status can change at any time. Be aware that even if a private site is not posted, this guide does not imply or suggest that collecting at the site is permitted.

Many sites in this book are in county parks, state forests, state parks, state game lands, federal lands, or other places that are accessible to the public, and while you can go to these sites, rock collecting is prohibited in many of these locations. However, rock-collecting rules are not applied uniformly in many cases. For instance, fossil collecting is allowed in some state parks in Pennsylvania, but mineral collecting is not. If you look at the park regulations, you will generally find that any form of ground disturbance, which technically includes simply picking up a rock, is strictly prohibited. However, many of these same parks have guides from state agencies on collecting fossils and minerals in the park. In these cases you will have to use your best judgment as to whether or not you are going to collect rocks if you visit a site. If there are signs clearly stating NO MINERAL COLLECTING, do not collect rocks. Likewise, if you are in a place where you know collecting is forbidden, you can enjoy seeing the rocks, but do not collect them.

Where an interesting mineral or fossil occurrence is on publically accessible land, but collecting is prohibited, I have still listed it in this book if I have been able to visit it and consider the locality worthy of a visit by anyone interested in rocks. Despite the efforts of some regulators, I have not yet found a site where it is against the law to look at the rocks.

In cases where I found localities that are clearly posted against trespassing, I have eliminated them from this book, unless they are a significant locality or a locality that is generally easy to get permission to access. For these sites, you must go the extra step to secure permission, or wait for an opportunity to take a field trip to the site with an established group. It is often a significant challenge to identify and get permission from the owner, which is why this book contains many other sites worth visiting, and I hope you'll consider visiting another site in the meantime.

I have also listed local attractions where appropriate. Many of these are local state parks, nearby lakes, and in some urban settings I have referenced nearby malls and cities. It is often a good idea to combine mineral and fossil field trips with other activities, as this makes the trip fair to other members of your group who may not have the slightest interest in rocks.

I know some readers will be disappointed that I did not include their favorite sites, while other readers will be relieved that I did not reveal their favorite site. If I inadvertently revealed your secret location, it could not have been too secret, as all of these sites are either mentioned in existing geologic literature or online or are very obvious when driving past the site. While I attempted to include as many sites as possible in this book, I found that the list of good sites kept growing, and eventually I had to draw the line on adding additional sites. The good news is that the more I kept looking, the more sites I found. This is important, as it shows that after even decades of rockhounding, there are still more sites to visit. I have never run out of potential places for looking at rocks. This book may be a good starting point in finding your own "hidden" site.

The best way to learn about rock collecting is to go out and look for rocks. You and your companions are bound to see some interesting geology and experience the scenery and adventure of going on a field trip, even if just for a morning or afternoon.

Rockhounding Basics

Rockhounding can be a low-budget hobby, especially when you are just starting out, as the entry requirements are relatively minimal. Literally all you need are your eyes and hands to see and pick up interesting rocks. However, as you advance, you'll want some additional tools.

Rockhounding Equipment

A good hammer is the most important tool for a rock hound. I recommend a rock pick hammer with a pointed tip. I have found them available at some surveying-supply shops and at rock shows. I have found it very difficult to find these in typical hardware stores, and you may have to order one online. My preferred brand is an Estwing foot-long hammer with a pointed tip and a Shock Reduction Grip®. I have used mine for over thirty years. It is almost impossible to destroy, despite thousands of whacks against very hard rocks and lots of time outside in the rain and snow.

Do not use a regular claw hammer. These will break apart quickly, and the steel that shoots off the hammer head when it hits a rock can be very dangerous. If you are hammering, it is also critical to wear safety glasses or goggles. I wear glasses normally to see, and my glasses have often been damaged by flying rock chips and steel. In the event that I am hammering large rocks on a constant basis, such as in a quarry, I will cover my glasses with safety goggles. When collecting in New Jersey, especially in urban environments, rocks are often associated with broken glass, which becomes another hazard when hit with a hammer. To be fair to New Jersey, I have this same problem in Pittsburgh, Harrisburg, and Philadelphia. I also use a chisel to help break apart rocks when needed, and I sometimes use a cheap flat-bladed screwdriver for soft shaly rocks where a chisel is too big to use.

Gloves are the next critical item. In the old days I used to do field work without gloves but realized quickly that it was a dangerous practice. Make sure you protect your hands. Get a good pair of heavy leather work gloves from your local hardware or big-box store. You will also find that gloves are great when traversing through briars, climbing on sharp rocks, and avoiding broken glass. It is also extremely easy to pinch your bare fingers when moving around large rocks, but gloves will help prevent the pinching. It is far better to get the end of your glove caught under a rock than the tip of your finger.

Get a good pair of steel-toed or equivalent boots to protect your feet. Having steel-toed boots is a requirement for collecting in quarries and mines, and it is very easy to find and purchase a good pair. I prefer to have relatively lightweight boots. Be sure to walk in them before purchasing to find a pair that fits comfortably.

A hard hat, while not needed for collecting at most roadcuts or places without overhead hazards, is equipment you should always have readily available. While you may not need one for casual rock collecting, you should have one with you or in your car in case you get invited to collect in a quarry or visit an active mine.

A field book is also very useful for recording key site information. I like to record coordinates of sites and take notes of what I have found for future reference. I also use a small pocket-size digital camera and often take hundreds of shots a day during a typical field trip. I never know what shots I am going to use until long after the trip. I often take repeated shots as my camera sometimes changes focus with movement and lighting, and I have a better chance of getting that perfect shot with more pictures.

A hand lens to inspect minerals and fossils up close is also very useful. I recommend getting a quality hand lens that is at least 10X magnification.

Carrying your rocks from the site is often a chore. I like to use a small backpack when I have to walk a long distance, but sometimes a five-gallon plastic bucket works best. A bucket is useful when you are picking up muddy rocks, and it is easy to put in your car. Just be careful to not break the bottom of the bucket if you intend to also use it for water. I have ruined several buckets with large, sharp rocks.

A wagon is also good to have if you are working in quarries or places where you can expect to take out significant amounts of rocks. If you go on a trip with a mineral club to a quarry, you can always tell who knows what they are doing, as they often come with a wagon to haul the rocks out of the pit. Collecting lots of rocks in a quarry is fine, as what you do not collect is just going to go to a crusher. However, if you go on a trip to an outcrop or small site and need to bring a wagon, you are collecting way too many rocks. Be considerate, and save some for the next visitor.

GPS Units and Maps

Before digital map technology became available, I used to find every site by using topographic and highway maps, but those days are long over. I now use a hand-held Global Positioning System (GPS) unit to record key site location information, and I use the coordinate feature on my car GPS to take me to the site. GPS devices are relatively common now, and many collectors have GPS smartphone apps. My GPS is still separate from my phone, and I like to record my locations by hand. However, I have used a smartphone in the field, and the satellite imagery, combined with real-time tracking, can be very helpful for finding difficult-to-locate sites. If you do not have GPS, I strongly recommend that you get one that helps you locate yourself in the field and gets you to the site. Keep in mind that current mapping technology will almost certainly be out of date within a few years, and you may want to supplement these recommendations with newer navigation methods.

Despite the advantages of GPS units and smartphones, you should always have maps as a backup. Batteries can die, and satellite and mobile signals can be dropped in the wilderness and urban areas where you do not have good clearance for satellite signals. A good highway map can be a relatively simple check for your GPS unit. If possible, you should also get topographic maps of your site. I consider the United States Geological Survey (USGS) 7.5 minute topographic quadrangles to be the best topographic maps for rockhounding. These are often referred to as 7.5-minute maps, as they cover 7.5 minutes of longitude and 7.5 minutes of latitude. The USGS is the primary civilian mapping agency of the government, and more than 55,000 of these 7.5-minute maps cover the lower 48 contiguous states. These maps are at a scale of 1:24,000, or 1 inch to 2,000 feet, which is an easy scale to work with, as it shows considerable detail while covering a wide area. I used to buy hard-copy maps, but I recently bought a set of topographic maps on CD for Pennsylvania and New Jersey through National Geographic. Now I can easily browse sites through my computer and just print the sections of the maps that I need.

Health and Safety

Rockhounding presents many hazards that you will not encounter in other hobbies. In addition to having the proper gear, there are many health and safety considerations. Any time you go into the field, you are going into an uncontrolled and potentially hostile environment, and you need to take some basic steps to protect yourself and your collecting companions.

Sunscreen is one of the most effective and easy-to-use safety products, but many collectors still ignore its benefits. However, you need to put it on right away after you get to the site, or even better, before you leave the house. Many sites, especially the floors of open pit mines, act like a giant solar reflector, and the sun can be very intense. I also highly recommend a good pair of dark **sunglasses.** I cannot spend any time at all in an area of light-colored rocks if I do not have my sunglasses. Likewise, if you are not wearing a hard **hat,** wear a baseball cap or other hat for protection from the sun.

Poison ivy can be a serious problem in Pennsylvania and New Jersey. If you do not know how to recognize poison ivy, I guarantee that you will become an expert after you get your first serious rash. Poison ivy usually grows on the borders of outcrops and rocks, and this is another good reason to wear gloves. In fact, if your gloves have had extensive contact with the poison ivy, you may just have to throw them away.

While I always enjoy collecting in shorts and short-sleeve shirts, many sites are hidden among briars and other plants that can make your experience miserable if your legs and arms are exposed. I recommend always having a pair of **long pants** and a **light jacket** available if you need it, and you can also anticipate that these clothes will get ripped up pretty badly by thorns, broken branches, and sharp rocks. Long pants and sleeves can also help protect you from the sun and insects.

Ticks are a major concern in the northeastern United States. I usually find that I have been exposed to ticks as I am driving away from the site and see several crawling on my arms and legs just as I am entering traffic. There is no worse motivation for a young or new rock hound than going home covered in ticks. Lyme disease is a serious issue, and you have to be on your guard at all times. The larger wood ticks, while not aesthetically pleasing, are typically not carriers of Lyme disease, while the much smaller deer ticks are known carriers. If you find a small tick embedded in you, and it has been there for more than 24 hours, you may be at risk for Lyme disease. Keep an eye on the bite mark and contact your physician if it gets worse over the next few days. Using an insect repellent that contains DEET is a good defense, as is light-colored clothing so you can quickly spot and remove the ticks. Insect repellant is also good to keep away the mosquitoes, which may be present at any sites near standing water. To remove a tick, grasp the skin around the insertion of the tick with a pair of fine-point tweezers and pull straight outward; be careful not to grasp the tick body, as it may inject germs into the skin.

I recommend an orange or yellow **safety vest** if you are collecting near a roadside. On the other hand, if you are collecting so close to a roadside that you need a safety vest, you probably should not be collecting at that site. No rock is worth getting hit by a car. But if you insist on collecting at a roadcut, get a safety vest.

Dehydration and hunger are trip spoilers. Make sure that you and your collecting companions bring enough bottled water, and if you will be out all day, bring something to eat. Nearly all of the sites in this guidebook are near cities and places to get lunch, and most trips are half-day trips, so hunger is generally not a problem. Water, on the other hand, can be a problem. I generally have at least one half liter of water in my backpack and often take two half liters of water, and make sure that my collecting companions also have water.

Getting to the site safely is important. The parking areas for the sites in this book can all be easily reached with a two-wheel-drive vehicle. It seems obvious, but if you are driving to a site, be sure your vehicle will get there and that you have plenty of gas. I always try to keep my tank topped off. This is not a big problem in Pennsylvania, but I know some parts of New Jersey, especially in the north, where everything, including gas stations, shut down by early evening. If you are taking more than one vehicle, make certain that there will be enough parking for two cars. Many drives are also very long, so if you get tired, be sure to pull over at a secure rest area and take a break.

While many collecting sites are in somewhat rural areas, some of the sites in this book are in urban settings. You should always **be aware of your surroundings,** make sure your vehicle is parked in a secure place, not leave valuables in your car, and be alert for suspicious characters. Generally, if you have a bad feeling about where you parked your car, you will find that feeling has been justified when you return.

Underground mines are generally a nonissue in Pennsylvania and New Jersey, as most of the unstable mines collapsed or were closed many decades ago, and many of the open mines now have bat gates or other structures that keep people out. However, it is still possible to come across open portals and shafts, especially in the iron-mining districts in the New Jersey Highlands. The best policy is to simply stay outside of any underground workings.

Finally, you have to be careful when dealing with sites on **private property.** Always ask permission, and be prepared to get yelled at or have other unpleasant experiences with the landowner. Many of my most unpleasant experiences have involved dealing with their large and quite vicious dogs.

Nearly all owners I have talked with have been good about giving permission, but every now and then I come across unfriendly owners. This comes with the hobby, so if you are going to look for rocks on private lands and ask their owners for access, you have to be ready to deal with difficult people.

Important Online Tools

Although many mineral and fossil localities have disappeared through development, it is much easier nowadays to access information to find new sites. I routinely run multiple searches through Google or Yahoo and use Google Earth and Google Maps to identify sites and to explore potential localities long before I get to the site.

I have purposely left website addresses out of this guide, as Internet addresses often expire, and generally it is much easier to find a web address via a search engine. Running an Internet search on a locality often brings up new and potentially important information updates, especially if a site has changed land status.

Likewise, all of the references cited in this book refer to the actual publication and do not provide a web address for access. However, if you type in the citation or key parts of it, you can often find them accessible online. If you cannot get access to them online, then you can generally get them through your state library. I have found that many publications are now only available on microfiche, but your librarian can often arrange for a copy to be emailed to you.

An interesting trend I have seen lately, based on many of my Internet searches, is that many sites that were once private land have become parklands or preserves. This has often opened them to public access. However, while they may now be open to the public, their new status as government land or a wildlife preserve will often preclude collecting or even touching rocks and minerals, as well as flowers, firewood, and practically everything else on the site. I have still listed many sites like this in the book, as you can still visit them, but be sure to research regulations before collecting.

Pennsylvania Geology

Some basic understanding of the geology of Pennsylvania will help you understand why you encounter certain rocks, minerals, and fossils in various parts of the state. Pennsylvania is a large state and has considerable variation in its geology, and nearly all rock types and geologic periods are represented to some extent. Pennsylvania can be roughly divided into six geologic provinces. These are the Atlantic Coastal Plain, Piedmont, New England, Ridge and Valley, Appalachian Plateaus, and the Central Lowlands. These provinces are further subdivided, but for our purposes, we are going to keep it simple and limit our list to the six main provinces.

Pennsylvania Atlantic Coastal Plain Province

This is one of the smallest provinces in Pennsylvania, and not surprisingly, it does not have much in the way of minerals. It is essentially the areas along the Delaware River in Bucks, Philadelphia, and Delaware Counties where alluvial sediments cover the bedrock. These sediments consist of clay, silt, sand, and gravel, and they were also deposited relatively recently compared to the underlying bedrock. If you are looking for minerals and fossils in Pennsylvania, your time is best spent elsewhere, but you will not have far to go. No rockhounding sites listed in this book occur in the Atlantic Coastal Plain Province.

Pennsylvania Piedmont Province

If you are in the Atlantic Coastal Plain Province and want to find minerals, you only have to go a short distance to reach the Piedmont Province, which is just to the west. This province consists of much older metamorphic and sedimentary rocks that have many of the most productive mineral-collecting areas in Pennsylvania. The Piedmont can be further divided into the Piedmont Uplands, the Piedmont Lowlands, and the Gettysburg-Newark Lowland, which is also often referred to as the Triassic Basin. The Piedmont Uplands consist mainly of schist and gneiss, which are among the oldest rocks in Pennsylvania. The Piedmont Lowlands consist of early Paleozoic sediments including sandstone, shale, and limestone, and generally these rocks are softer and more easily eroded than the rocks in the Uplands. The Gettysburg-Newark Lowland consists of Triassic sediments and intrusive rocks, which are principally diabase. As the rocks in the Gettysburg-Newark Lowland are mainly sediments, this province is often referred to as the Triassic Basin. Many rock and mineral sites are found in the Piedmont Province, but fossils are practically absent except for some minor exceptions in Triassic rocks.

Pennsylvania New England Province

This is an unfortunate name, as Pennsylvania does not even border New England. It is also referred to as the Reading Prong, which is a much better name, as at least Reading is in Pennsylvania. This province consists mainly of granitic gneiss, granodiorite, and quartzite, which are very resistant to erosion. The hills of this province are higher than the surrounding sedimentary rocks of the Piedmont Lowlands and Valley and Ridge Province, and the slopes are often quite steep. Quarries and exposures in roadcuts in this province can sometime yield some interesting minerals, but as you would expect in igneous and metamorphic rocks, fossils are absent.

Pennsylvania Ridge and Valley Province

The Ridge and Valley Province comprises classic Pennsylvania geology. Long before satellite photos were common, one could look at a Pennsylvania highway map or a relief map from an atlas and see distinct patterns in the mountains and valleys of central Pennsylvania. The patterns are the result of folded sequences of middle to later Paleozoic sediments including shale, sandstone, siltstone, and limestone. The more resistant sandstones form the ridges, while the softer limestones and shales form the valleys. This province has been further subdivided into several other regions, but for the purposes of this book, we just need to know the general location of the province. This province often offers excellent fossil collecting, especially in some of the Devonian sediments. Minerals that occur in this province generally formed through sedimentary processes and precipitation through near-surface interactions with the rocks and groundwater. Some of these secondary minerals that can be found in the Ridge and Valley Province include malachite, turquoise, wavellite, and goethite.

Pennsylvania Appalachian Plateaus Province

The Appalachian Plateaus Province is the next major geologic province to the west and north of the Ridge and Valley Province. This province generally consists of nearly horizontal late Paleozoic rocks, and these are principally siltstones and sandstones with minor sequences of shales, coal, and limestone. The Plateaus Province, as it is generally higher in elevation than the other provinces, has often been deeply incised by streams and rivers as the waterways have continually been cutting away at the soft sediments. Parts of the northern section of this province were once covered with glaciers, and this resulted in the deposition of glacial sediments over much of the bedrock in these areas. This province has also been subdivided into many sections. This area has many fossil locations, and mineral collecting generally consists of secondary minerals that formed as nodules or concretions in the sedimentary rocks.

Pennsylvania Central Lowlands Province

This is northwestern Pennsylvania's counterpart to the Atlantic Coastal Plain Province, but the sediments are mostly glacial in origin. This is a narrow band of unconsolidated sediments deposited as the glaciers in the area retreated. The streams that flow into Lake Erie are generally perpendicular to the shoreline, and they have cut through these sediments to expose the underlying bedrock and often form very scenic canyons. The sediments do not offer much in the way of minerals, but there are some interesting cone-in-cone sediments in the underlying bedrock, which is actually part of the Appalachian Plateau Province, as well as some fossiliferous rocks exposed in the bedrock of the streams. No rockhounding sites listed in this book occur in the Central Lowlands Province.

Pennsylvania Natural Resources

Pennsylvania has tremendous natural resources, which have had a profound effect on the development of the United States and the world. Pennsylvania is a very large state and is geographically positioned to serve many large markets for raw materials and energy. This has provided the basis for its rich manufacturing heritage, which continues today. Many mines and quarries may no longer be operating, but they contributed a great deal to the economy when they were active, and in many cases literally provided the foundation for many of the roads, factories, and businesses in Pennsylvania. When collecting minerals and fossils, it is important to understand the underlying reasons for the location of mines and quarries. This will often help you identify the types of rocks you will encounter and give you some lessons in history at the same time.

Iron

Iron was the first metal to be exploited in Pennsylvania. The iron industry in Pennsylvania dates back to the 1700s, when iron was mined to supply cannon and shot for the Revolutionary War. Iron deposits in Pennsylvania can be roughly classified as sedimentary, meta-sedimentary, and contact metamorphic deposits. The sedimentary deposits include goethite-limonite and bog iron, "Clinton-type" hematitic sediments, and siderite-limonite rocks. The term Clinton refers to Clinton, New York, where the deposits were mined for iron, and Clinton-type has been applied to describe similar hematitic sandstone deposits around the world. The meta-sedimentary deposits include magnetite and hematite in metamorphosed Precambrian through Ordovician iron-rich sediments. The contact metamorphic iron deposits are commonly referred to as "Cornwall-type" deposits after the large iron mine near Cornwall, Pennsylvania.

Iron furnaces were developed throughout Pennsylvania to process the numerous small deposits of iron ores found near the surface in many areas of the state. Many of the limonitic bog iron-type deposits in southeastern Pennsylvania were important iron supplies during the Civil War. Today, many of these deposits are long gone and covered up by urban development, lakes, or on private grounds, but some remnants still provide interesting collecting sites for iron mineralization.

The iron furnace deposits were generally small and soon largely worked out, and many of the larger deposits were soon mined. The deposit at Cornwall, located in southeastern Pennsylvania, was developed into a major open-pit iron mine. This was the largest deposit of iron in the United States east of Lake Superior, and at one time was reported to be the largest open-pit mine in the world. An airborne magnetometer survey led to the discovery of the Grace Mine near Morgantown in southeast Pennsylvania in 1947, and this was soon developed into another large iron mine. America's appetite for iron and steel seemed insatiable, but technology to develop the vast iron resources of the Lake Superior mines, combined with other supplies from around the world, soon doomed both Pennsylvania's iron mines and much of the steel industry in the state. The Cornwall mines never were reopened after they flooded during Hurricane Agnes in 1972, and the Grace Mine closed afterward in 1977. Today, some limited collecting can be done around Cornwall, and the Grace Mine is only accessible with permission. Former iron mines in Pennsylvania offer many mineral-collecting opportunities, including goethite, magnetite, hematite, and associated host rock minerals such as garnet and feldspars.

Coal

Coal is one of the principal natural resources in Pennsylvania. The coal industry in Pennsylvania started with anthracite mining in the early 1800s. Anthracite, which is a hard, dense coal, was discovered in the mountains of northeastern Pennsylvania, and this discovery came at a time when energy for steam and heat for houses was much in demand. The early days of the industry had to focus on transporting the coal to market, and many of the first major coal-mining companies started with transporting coal down rivers and canals, and later by railroads. It was a tough, brutal industry, and the lack of modern technology made it extremely dangerous. Much of the work was underground, and many of the coal seams were in tightly folded rocks, which often made the mines extremely unstable. Coal dust, methane, and other hazards made for both chronic problems such as black lung and acute problems such as explosions. However, the demand for coal resulted in jobs for many and some degree of prosperity for a few.

The anthracite industry later gave way to the bituminous coal industry, which is located mainly in the Plateau regions of north-central and western Pennsylvania. Bituminous coal is much softer and was generally found in rocks that lay horizontal and hence were more predictable. The great coal seams like the Pittsburgh Coal in western Pennsylvania ultimately provided vast riches for a very select group and helped fuel the Pennsylvania steel and electrical-generation industries. While the anthracite industry is all but gone, bituminous mining in Pennsylvania is still going strong and will continue until the mines are completely played out or until we find an energy source that is better than coal.

Coal has left significant environmental degradation in Pennsylvania. Acid-mine drainage has killed many streams, and the vast landfills of fly ash, which is the residue from burning coal, still leach contaminants into streams and groundwater. However, the waste piles from many former coal mines are being used as fuel for electrical power generation in Pennsylvania, and many acid-mine drainage sites have been cleaned up. Pennsylvania has made tremendous progress in fixing the environmental damage from this industry, and the lessons learned have helped further protect the environment as new industries are developed in Pennsylvania. Many former coal mines offer unique fossil-collecting opportunities, especially for plant fossils.

Oil and Natural Gas

Pennsylvania is the birthplace of the American oil industry, with oil first drilled near Titusville in 1857. The region quickly became a boomtown, and the early oil industry had virtually no environmental or market controls. So many wells were drilled that the price of oil plummeted, and those in the oil industry got to experience the first of the boom-and-bust cycles that are so characteristic of the oil business. This set the stage for the Standard Oil Company to enter the picture, and Standard Oil soon managed to control the entire industry, until it was broken up under the Sherman Antitrust Act in 1911. In the meantime, the great oil discovery at Spindletop in Texas in 1901 had produced much more oil for the market, and Pennsylvania crude was no longer the dominant source of oil for the United States. Later discoveries in the United States and elsewhere in the world further drove the Pennsylvania oil industry down. Oil is still drilled and refined in Pennsylvania, and the industry is much more efficient and environmentally responsible, but it is still subject to the booms and busts of our modern economy.

In the past few years, Pennsylvania has taken a lead role in the production of deep shale natural gas. Natural gas was encountered in the early days of the oil industry in Pennsylvania, but the production was generally limited and confined to small and relatively shallow wells. The Marcellus and other black shales were long known to contain natural gas, but it was not until recently that improved techniques in horizontal drilling and hydraulic fracturing enabled development of shale gas in Pennsylvania on a large scale. Shale gas is having a tremendous effect on the economy of Pennsylvania and surrounding states, and it is being developed nationwide and around the world in other shales. The United States, once perceived as being shortchanged when it came to natural gas reserves, may now well have some of the most significant gas reserves on the planet, and Pennsylvania is a key player in shale gas. From a mineral- and fossil-collecting standpoint, natural gas development does not offer much in the way of new sites, but new access roads and better geologic information will be a likely result of natural gas development and may lead to some new collecting sites.

Construction Aggregates and Cement

Construction aggregates and cement are the lifeblood of the construction industry. Pennsylvania is a leader in construction aggregate and cement production as the state has vast reserves of high-quality crystalline rocks, sandstone, and limestone. While the state has a great deal of stone, the environmental and permitting issues with opening a new aggregate or cement rock source are often prohibitive, so the sites with current mining permits and high-quality reserves have often dramatically increased in value. Since the main cost associated with aggregates is transportation, the markets for stone are often local, and cement is also expensive to transport. Since the market is local, you can often see the local geology reflected in the building materials of the roads and buildings of the towns near the quarries. For instance, many of the roads in eastern Pennsylvania have a distinct reddish cast, and this comes from the reddish-brown Triassic sediments that are a local source of aggregate. In Hummelstown many of the buildings are made of brownstone, which was once a locally mined building stone. While quarries provide great opportunities for rock collecting, active mines often require advance permission and often can only be entered through a group or club. Abandoned quarries on state or publically owned ground, provided they are accessible and safe, also often offer some unique opportunities to see minerals and fossils.

New Jersey Geology

New Jersey has a diverse geologic history, and nearly all geologic periods are represented in the state. New Jersey can also be divided into physiographic provinces to better understand what you will encounter when looking for rocks. The four principal provinces are the Coastal Plain, the Piedmont, the Highlands, and the Valley and Ridge.

New Jersey Coastal Plain Province

This is the largest province in New Jersey. It covers the southeastern part of the state south of the Fall Zone, which can be roughly defined as a line between Trenton and Woodbridge. The rocks in this zone are principally unconsolidated coastal sediments and some consolidated Tertiary and Cretaceous-age sediments. Many of the coastal sediments were mined for glass and foundry sands. Minerals in this area are generally limited to hematite, quartz, and authigenic minerals such as vivianite, and fossils can also be found in some of the Cretaceous sediments.

New Jersey Piedmont Province

The New Jersey Piedmont Province is just northwest of the Coastal Plain Province and consists mainly of Triassic and early Jurassic rocks. The Triassic sedimentary rocks are part of the Newark Supergroup, which is a thick sequence of poorly sorted nonmarine sediments that outcrop along the eastern United States and into Canada. The Piedmont also has numerous early Jurassic dikes and sills, including the Palisades Sill, which forms the Palisades Cliffs along the Hudson River. This province has several interesting mineral occurrences, including zeolite minerals in the Jurassic basalts, carnelian agate that has weathered from the basalts and is now found in stream gravels, and copper mineralization in some of the Triassic sediments.

New Jersey Highlands Province

Northwest of the Piedmont is the Highlands Province, which has the oldest rocks in New Jersey. The rocks include Precambrian granites and gneisses and early Paleozoic carbonates and clastic rocks. This is the most mineral-rich part of the state. The area had extensive zinc and iron mines, and many of the carbonates were also metamorphosed into very hard marbles that made outstanding aggregates. The area also has many other quarries that extracted other hard and durable crystalline rocks of the province. Most of the well-known rock and mineral sites in New Jersey are found in this province.

New Jersey Valley and Ridge Province

Confined to the northwestern corner of the state, this is the smallest province in New Jersey and is an extension of the Ridge and Valley Province in Pennsylvania. The area has tightly folded sediments and prominent southwest–northeast-trending ridges and valleys, but it does not have coal deposits like those found in parts of the Valley and Ridge in Pennsylvania. This is a relatively undeveloped area and is likely to remain so, given the protections given to the nearby national park at the Delaware Water Gap and the local restrictions to development. The area has some unique mineralization, such as the copper in Silurian rocks near the Delaware River, but this area is off-limits to collecting. However, there are some sections outside of the national park that offer the opportunity to see quartz crystals and fossils.

New Jersey Natural Resources

Modern New Jersey has an economy that is based on services, information technology, manufacturing, chemicals, and government. Much of this industry was made possible by the basic materials such as metals and industrial minerals found in New Jersey. Even the tourist industry, which I classify under services, owes a lot to New Jersey's mining history. Many tourist attractions in the New Jersey Highlands include former zinc and iron mines, and the Jersey shore would be nothing without sand. The metal mines have long since closed, and many industrial mineral deposits, especially the older aggregate quarries, have also closed, but they provided the foundation for present-day New Jersey. Understanding what was once mined here can help you find collecting sites.

Zinc

The zinc industry was a huge part of the economy of many towns in northern New Jersey, and the zinc mines are especially famous for their unique minerals, many of which are fluorescent. The zinc ores were first worked for iron, which is not surprising as one of the main zinc minerals, franklinite, strongly resembles magnetite. However, attempts to get iron from the zinc ores with standard iron processing were futile and must have been a nightmare for the first metallurgists in New Jersey. Later the ores were correctly identified and processed as zinc ores, and the timing was excellent as the developing economy of the United States needed zinc for paint, batteries, and alloys. Zinc was mined in New Jersey until 1986, when the last great underground zinc mine at Sterling Hill in Ogdensburg was finally shut down permanently due to low prices for zinc. Zinc minerals from New Jersey are popular among collectors worldwide due to their fluorescence and the fact that similar occurrences are not found anywhere else in the world.

Iron and Copper

The New Jersey iron industry was active from approximately 1760 to the 1870s. The raw iron ores included both hematitic bog iron ores from the Coastal Plain Province and magnetite ores from the Highlands Province. Much of the fuel for iron furnaces was charcoal, and in the second half of the 1800s, anthracite and bituminous coal became the fuel for iron mines to the west in Pennsylvania. The iron mines in New Jersey could not compete as they did not have similar access to coal, and the mines and furnaces soon closed. Many of the former iron mines offer some interesting opportunities to find both magnetite and bog iron ore, but many of the mines have either been reclaimed, are on private land, or are in areas where collecting is prohibited.

Copper mining was a rather disappointing industry in New Jersey. The Schuyler copper mine in North Arlington, which was first worked in the early 1700s, was one of the first metal mines in North America. The Pahaquarry copper mines near the Delaware River were reportedly worked as early as the 1660s. None of the copper deposits in New Jersey were very large, and while some profits were made in the early years of mining, much effort was later spent in chasing ores that proved nonexistent. Successful copper mining requires properly timed and significant investments, metallurgical expertise, and most importantly, ores with abundant copper. The New Jersey copper deposits could never be economically developed. During World War II, copper was in much demand, but even that demand, coupled with the favorable geographic location near potential refining centers, could not make up for the relative lack of copper in New Jersey mineral deposits. Today the remaining mines and areas of mineralization offer some interesting collecting opportunities, but nearly all of them are on private land or public land where collecting is prohibited.

Sand

New Jersey has a large sand industry, and all of the sand comes from the southern half of the state in the Coastal Plain Province. Sand is mined for glass sand, the foundry industry for casting molds, water treatment and filtration, the construction industry, and even for the sports industry for baseball infields and football fields. While the glass-sand industry has declined significantly, high-quality New Jersey sand is still in demand for many specialty applications. The sand is all mined aboveground, and often the former sand quarries are reclaimed as lakes and other valuable wildlife habitat. From a mineral-collecting standpoint, sand is not terribly interesting, but it still is useful to know how sand plays a part in the mineral industry of New Jersey.

Construction Aggregates

Construction aggregates are big business in New Jersey. Many of the largest quarries in New Jersey are located in the Highlands Province, as this area has the largest extent of hard, durable rocks. Since aggregates are also local to their markets due to transportation expenses, there are also numerous aggregate sources in the other provinces. The demand for aggregate during boom times often resulted in numerous small quarries as well, and some of these, which have long been abandoned, can also be excellent places to observe and collect minerals. In addition, many of the large railroad cuts, building-foundation excavations, and other large excavations were used as aggregate sources, and many of these offer excellent collecting when you can get access.

How to Use This Guide

The sites in this book are listed by their location in the physiographic provinces. In Pennsylvania, the sites are generally numbered westward from Philadelphia. In New Jersey, the sites are generally numbered eastward from the Philadelphia area.

Site names are often based on the nearest town, but in some cases I have used a local geographic feature for the locality name, especially if this will help collectors with locating the site. I have also included Pennsylvania and New Jersey maps with county names and the localities plotted on both maps so you can better plan your collecting trips.

The site descriptions will let you know what to expect during your visit. The **site type** refers to the type of occurrence, and this generally is a physical description of the site, which may be a streambed, roadcut, former quarry, or outcrop. The **land status** is based on the best available information and should let you know if you will be able to access the site without special permission or if you may need to secure approval from a site owner for access.

Roadcuts are often in the **highway right-of-way,** which is a general term for the easement along a public road that is reserved by the highway department or other government agency for future road expansions, utilities, and other features that may be constructed along the road. In general these right-of-ways can be accessed by rockhounds, but you must be certain to stay out of areas that are clearly posted against trespassing. In some states the highway department has also made it very clear that collecting is not allowed on certain roadsides. If you see a sign that indicates that access along the side of a highway or roadside is prohibited, stay away.

The **material** refers to the type of minerals, rocks, or fossils that a visitor would likely find of most interest at a particular site. If they are listed, I can assure you that they are present at the site, but it still may take some effort to find them. In some cases if a mineral or fossil is reported to be present at a site and I did not find it, I have listed it as "reported" if the geologic conditions are appropriate for that mineral or fossil to be present. Just because I did not find it does not mean it is not there.

The **host rock** is the rock in which the material is found, and I have generally named the geologic formation or type of rock that best describes the enclosing rocks as the host rock. It is important to understand what rocks host your materials of interest as you can use this knowledge to find similar sites.

The **difficulty** level is a guide to the likelihood of finding or observing the materials referenced in the site description. Some sites are loaded with material and you can step onto the site and find as much as you could possibly desire. Other sites take hours and hours of effort to find a single specimen, and even your most diligent efforts are not a guarantee that you will find or observe anything. If a site is marked as difficult, be aware that it may not be a good site for impatient collectors.

The **family-friendly** rating is very subjective and depends entirely upon your family. If the description says "yes" without any qualifiers, you will generally find this to be a site where you can take family members that can handle moderate walking and want to look at rocks. These sites also tend to be among the easier sites to find rocks. If the description says "no," generally this is because the minerals or fossils are very hard to find, or because site access is very limited or difficult. I have also included a section on **special concerns** so you know why this may not be a good site for everyone, especially if you are bringing small children. This does not mean you should not take your family, but be prepared to deal with the issues mentioned in the site description.

Tools needed refers to the rockhounding equipment that you should have for visiting a particular site. A good way to spoil a trip is to bring only a rock hammer when you also needed to bring a digging bar and a chisel, or to find out that you really needed to bring a bucket to bring home rocks that are covered in black clay. While a rock hammer is a good general tool, having the right additional implements can often make the difference between success and failure for a trip.

I have included **special attractions** for nearly all of the sites in this book, as it is very important to know your surroundings and visit other interesting nearby places when out rockhounding. Combining rockhounding trips with other non-rockhounding experiences is often a good way to keep your companions interested, especially if they are like many of my family members that want to do anything but look at more rocks.

Each of the rockhounding locations in this book has **GPS** coordinates for parking, and if necessary a GPS coordinate for the site, in the event you must walk to the site. The coordinates are provided in degrees, minutes, and seconds and use the World Geodetic System (WGS 84) datum. The coordinates are rounded to the nearest second. Enter the coordinates in your GPS device, and they will take your vehicle on a route to the site. However, be aware that some GPS systems will take you on back roads and trails, and these may not be the best routes to the site. In some cases, especially in rural areas, they may take you on roads and trails that may not even be made for motor vehicles. You should always have a state highway map at a minimum for backup.

Lastly, I have also listed the **topographic quadrangle(s)** in which the site is located. The topographic quadrangle can often give you key information about the area surrounding the site and let you know in advance what significant features are at the site, such as steep topography, lakes, swamps, or cultural features such as buildings or roads. While it is not critical to have the topographic map if you have a road map and GPS coordinates, it is often useful. As described earlier, it is now possible to buy topographic maps on CD, and in some cases you can also access them on line, so it is no longer necessary to have a library of hard-copy topographic maps.

Do not assume that this guide gives you permission to collect or to access the property. In general, all public sites in this guide can be accessed and you can look at the rocks, but many parks and government sites do not allow the collecting or disturbing of rocks. If the site is private, do not enter posted areas without obtaining permission, and be aware that some private ground is not often clearly posted against trespassing. In many areas ownership and the rules regarding rock collecting are not clear, so if collecting regulations are unclear at any of these sites, leave your hammer in the car and just enjoy looking at the rocks.

PENNSYLVANIA SITES

1. Prospect Park Kyanite

This piece of kyanite was found at this site in June 2001.

County: Delaware
Site type: Loose rocks in small creek bed
Land status: Private property near apartment complex and ballfield, not posted
Material: Kyanite, light-blue and dark-gray blades
Host rock: Cobbles and boulders of coarse Wissahickon schist with zones of kyanite
Difficulty: Moderate
Family-friendly: No, site is too close to apartments, lots of potentially hazardous junk in creek
Tools needed: Hammer, gloves, boots, bucket
Special concerns: Creek is small, access uncertain, area very picked over as of 2012. Creek is also full of broken glass, metal, and other items that may pose hazards.
Special attractions: Philadelphia
GPS for parking: N39° 52' 44" / W75° 18' 16"

The creek is generally very small, and you can find kyanite on the banks and within the creek.

Topographic quadrangle: Landsdowne, PA

Finding the site: Take I-95 to exit 9B to PA 420, and head north across Darby Creek. From I-95, proceed approximately 0.6 mile to Lazaretto Road. Turn right onto Lazaretto Road, immediately turn left into an apartment complex, and park there. The kyanite is found in the small creek next to the apartments. Alternatively, you can also park near the baseball field on the opposite side of PA 420 and access the creek from this area.

Rockhounding

This small creek is an unnamed tributary to Darby Creek. The creek basin drains areas that are underlain by Precambrian Wissahickon schist, and some zones of this schist have kyanite, which subsequently washes into this tributary. Kyanite is an aluminum silicate (Al_2SiO_5) that often forms bright-blue elongated crystals, and large specimens that are bright "electric" blue are often highly prized by collectors.

The kyanite is found by walking along the creek and observing rocks for flashes of light blue or blade-shaped crystals that may indicate kyanite.

If you go to this locality, make sure you have good boots and gloves. As in most urban localities, the creek is filled with broken glass and pieces of metal, and the water is undoubtedly full of oil and bacteria-laden stormwater runoff. This is a relatively well-known collecting site, and while it is always worth visiting, during my latest visit in April 2012, I found the site very picked over and was not able to find any good blue kyanite. However, a lot depends on how much time you have and how hard you look, so I am optimistic that there is still kyanite to be found, it is just not that easy anymore. It may be worthwhile to explore other areas further upstream.

References: Beard, 2001; Stepanski and Snow, 2000

Sites 1–6

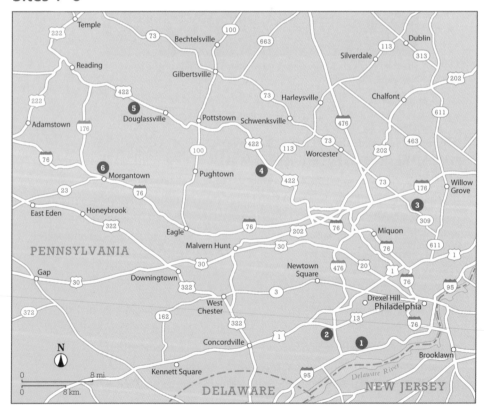

2. Smedley Park Apatite

The apatite crystals are small but their blue-green color makes them easy to spot in the pegmatitic rocks.

See map page 28.

County: Delaware

Site type: Pegmatitic rocks in Crum Creek

Land status: Delaware County Park property, public access, but mineral collecting may not be allowed

Material: Green-blue apatite crystals in pegmatitic rocks

Host rock: Pegmatites that have intruded the Baltimore gneiss and Wissahickon schist

Difficulty: Moderate

Family-friendly: Yes

Tools needed: Hammer, chisel, bucket, hand lens

Special concerns: If crossing Crum Creek, you will have to deal with significant logs and brush, but there is a trail to the site that does not require crossing the creek.

Special attractions: Smedley Park

GPS for parking: N39° 55' 11" / W75° 21' 48"

GPS for pegmatitic boulders in Crum Creek: N39° 55' 26" / W75° 21' 38"

Topographic quadrangle: Landsdowne, PA

Finding the site: Take I-476 to exit 3, which is for US 13, aka the East Baltimore Pike. Take the East Baltimore Pike east, proceed approximately 0.3 mile, and turn north onto Paper Mill Road, which is the first north road east of the exit 3 intersection. Paper Mill Road leads into Smedley Park. Follow this approximately 0.6 mile to the end of the road, and park in the parking lot. From there, walk upstream along Crum Creek. The best trail is on the east side of the creek. If you start on the west side, you will have to cross numerous logs and brush in Crum Creek. About 2,500 feet upstream from the parking area, you will see some large white boulders in the streambed—this is the pegmatitic boulder site.

Rockhounding

This site is referred to as a beryl locality in the 1969 edition of *Mineral Collecting in Pennsylvania,* but I have never been able to conclusively find beryl at this site. However, I have found small blue-green crystals of apatite in the white granitic pegmatite boulders in Crum Creek. The boulders with the apatite are in a broad, flat section of the creek, and they are much lighter in color than the surrounding rocks in the area. You will also see many previous signs of rock hounds at this

The pegmatitic boulders are found within the creek bed, and they are easy to spot as they are much lighter in color than the surrounding dark gneisses and schists.

site, which mainly consist of freshly broken rocks on top of the boulders. Look for coarse zones in the pegmatitic rocks, break them apart, and check for the tiny blue-green apatite crystals. A hand lens is very helpful at this site. The blue-green of the apatite contrasts well against the light-tan to white feldspar and quartz of the pegmatites. In addition, outcrops of silvery mica schist are just east of the parking area near the south bank of Crum Creek. Please note that this is a county park, so mineral collecting may not be allowed, but you are certainly welcome to look at the rocks. I say "may not" as a sign near the entrance summarizes typical park rules (no guns, no alcohol, no narcotics) but does not specifically state "no mineral collecting."

Reference: Lapham et al., 1969

3. Oreland Goethite

The goethite is easy to spot as it is nearly black, shiny, and often has a botryoidal texture.

See map page 28.

County: Montgomery

Site type: Streambed

Land status: Private, western part of creek not posted

Material: Loose pieces of goethite in streambed

Host rock: Alluvial stream gravels, no outcrops

Difficulty: Easy

Family-friendly: Yes

Tools needed: Hammer, but most specimens are loose in streambed and do not require trimming

Special concerns: Suburban setting so noise must be minimal (no loud rock hammering), site may become posted against access at any time

Special attractions: King of Prussia Mall, Franklin Mills Mall

The goethite pieces are found as loose rocks in this dry stream bed.

GPS parking: N40° 6' 45" / W75° 11' 28"
GPS streambed with goethite: N40° 6' 46" / W75° 11' 34"
Topographic quadrangle: Germantown, PA
Finding the site: From the Pennsylvania Turnpike, take exit 26 to PA 309 South, and then proceed approximately 1.5 miles to PA 73 South, Continue on PA 73 South 0.8 mile to Oreland Mill Road. This is shown as "Five Points" on the Germantown topographic quadrangle. The juncture of Oreland Mill Road and PA 73 is a difficult intersection to navigate, as it has five intersecting roads, and the turn onto Oreland Mill Road is to the left and at a severe angle. It may be advisable to continue on PA 73 and turn around to make this turn onto Oreland Mill Road. Once you are on Oreland Mill Road, continue northwest approximately 0.4 mile, turn right onto Meadow Lane and park. Walk north to the small bridge on Oreland Mill Road that is over a dry creek. At the time of a site visit in January 2012, the eastern part of the creek was posted as private property, but the western part was not posted. I suspect that landowners east of the bridge got tired of rock collectors walking up and down the creek.

Rockhounding

This dry streambed has abundant pieces of black botryoidal goethite that often have a radiating, fiber-like texture on freshly broken surfaces. Goethite is an iron hydroxide mineral and was an important source of iron ore in Colonial times. The goethite formed as nodules in the underlying bedrock of the Cambrian-age Ledger, Elbrook, and Ordovician-Cambrian-age Conestoga Formations. These nodules weathered out of the bedrock and are found in this dry streambed, along with large pieces of quartz and other pieces from the underlying bedrock. The site is unique in that there are no outcrops. Loose pieces of black to dark-brown botryoidal goethite can be spotted in the streambed and picked up, and cracking the larger pieces open often reveals the fiber-like character of the goethite. As mentioned above, the eastern part of the creek has been posted as private property. In the event the western side of the property also becomes posted, it is likely that sections of the creek downstream from posted areas, if they are accessible, may also have goethite, as the goethite is continually washed downstream as it weathers out of the bedrock.

References: Beard, 2004; Gordon, 1922

4. Phoenixville Dolomite Crystals

Excellent crystalline displays can be made by some rock trimming with your hammer.

See map page 28.

County: Chester

Site type: Boulders next to railroad tracks and river

Land status: Private but not posted

Material: Orange dolomite/ankerite crystals on dolomitic boulders

Host rock: Dolomitic boulders, but no rock is in outcrop

Difficulty: Easy

Family-friendly: Yes, but be careful of traffic and trains on rail tracks

Tools needed: Hammer, gloves, bucket

Special concerns: Traffic when crossing Bridge Street, trains, ticks

Special attractions: None

GPS parking: N40° 08' 07" / W75° 30' 33"

GPS boulder area: N40° 08' 03" / W75° 30' 33"

Topographic quadrangle: Phoenixville, PA

Finding the site: Phoenixville can be a confusing town for driving, so a map and a GPS unit are recommended. Take PA 23, aka Nutt Road to Manavon Street, aka PA 29. Turn northeast on Manavon Street, continue 0.2 mile, and turn northwest onto Starr Street. Take Starr Street approximately 0.6 mile, and it ends at a T. Turn right (northeast) onto Bridge Street, and proceed about 500 feet. The parking area for the site is on the west side of PA 29 just before you cross the Schuylkill River.

The dolomitic boulders with the crystals are adjacent to the railroad tracks.

Rockhounding

This site does not have any outcrops but has some orange-brown dolomite crystals on boulders and rocks between the railroad tracks and the Schuylkill River. The boulders were brought to the area for fill or to construct a berm along the rail line. At the time of my visit, the main pile had apparently been removed, but some smaller boulders, which are still very large, could be found along the tree line by the railroad tracks. The dolomite boulders are not part of the bedrock, as the bedrock in this area is mapped as Triassic Stockton Formation, which is a dark-red to brown arkosic sandstone. The dolomite crystals might be the iron-bearing variety of dolomite known as ankerite, which has the chemical formula $CaFe(CO_3)_2$. Ankerite is similar to dolomite except that it is yellowish brown to brown instead of white to gray, and it is common in iron-bearing formations. The collecting area is on the northeast side of the railroad tracks opposite the Columbia Station, which is now a banquet hall. The rock pile extends a few hundred feet to the southeast, and the sides of many of the boulders and rocks have surfaces with well-formed crystals. Some of the crystals are up to 0.3 inch in diameter. The rocks with the crystals were right on the surface, and I only used my hammer for trimming specimens. I highly recommend sturdy work gloves as the dolomitic rocks are heavy and it is easy to pinch fingers when turning over the larger rocks.

References: Beard, 2007; Stepanski and Snow, 2000

5. Hay Creek Prehnite and Stilbite

The prehnite often occurs as veins in the diabase host rock.

See map page 28.
County: Berks
Site type: Outcrop along trail and rocks in streambed
Land status: Township land, hiking trail, not posted
Material: Light-green prehnite in outcrop and stilbite on rocks in streambed
Host rock: Triassic diabase
Difficulty: Easy
Family-friendly: Yes, as it has a hiking trail and Hay Creek and is very scenic
Tools needed: Hammer, chisel
Special concerns: Ticks, may have to get wet when crossing Hay Creek
Special attractions: Reading pagoda
GPS parking: N40° 15' 13" / W75° 48' 50"
GPS outcrop with prehnite: N40° 14' 59" / W75° 49' 11.1"
Topographic quadrangles: Birdsboro and Elverson, PA
Finding the site: From US 422, take the exit going south through Birdsboro, which is South Center Road/PA 345. Continue south on PA 345 for approximately

The outcrop with prehnite is on the south side of the trail near Hay Creek.

1.2 miles. South Center Road then becomes North and South Furnace Streets, which then become Hay Creek Road. Continue to the end of Hay Creek Road, which is approximately 1.2 miles from where South Center Road ended. Hay Creek Road ends at a wide gravel parking area, and parking is on the right side of the road along Hay Creek. After you park, simply walk across Hay Creek and hike south on the former road. You will cross an old bridge over Hay Creek, and the outcrop with the prehnite is approximately 1,500 feet further south on your left. The outcrop is on the south side of the old road and on the south side of Hay Creek. You may also be able to approach the Hay Creek area from the former SR 82 south of Birdsboro, which will require taking several back roads. but this route is not recommended unless you are familiar with the area.

Rockhounding

This locality has an established parking area and a walking trail. You have to cross Hay Creek to get to the trail, so you can expect to get wet. Many people use this trail for walking dogs, fishing, and accessing rock climbing in the area. Rocks with stilbite and other minerals such as byssolite and calcite can be found in the bed of Hay Creek. Like many places in Pennsylvania, ticks are a potential problem at this site. I was bit by a Lyme disease–carrying tick during a trip to this site in the summer of 2007 and had to receive antibiotic treatments (yes, two treatments, one was not enough), so be especially careful in this area.

References: Beard, 2008; Gordon, 1922; MacLachlan, 1992

6. Morgantown Stromatolitic Cambrian Carbonates

This large outcrop shows abundant stromatolites.

See map page 28.
County: Berks
Site type: Roadcut
Land status: Private, not posted, may be in road right-of-way
Material: Stromatolitic limestone
Host rock: Cambrian carbonates of the Conococheague Formation
Difficulty: Easy
Family-friendly: No, too close to traffic
Tools needed: Hammer, gloves
Special concerns: Traffic and ticks
Special attractions: French Creek State Park
GPS parking: N40° 09' 32" / W75° 52' 39"

This stromatolitic piece was found loose on top of the hill above the outcrops.

Topographic quadrangle: Morgantown, PA

Finding the site: From the Pennsylvania Turnpike (I-76), take exit 298 and proceed west and then south on PA 10 back under the turnpike and into Morgantown. This is a distance of approximately 1.5 miles. Turn left (east) on PA 23, aka East Main Street, continue approximately 0.5 mile, then turn left (north) on Morgan Way, and go back under the turnpike. The outcrops and a small parking area are on the west side of Morgan Way just south of the intersection with Quarry Road, approximately 0.2 mile northeast of PA 23.

Rockhounding

The area is described as within the Millbach member of the Cambrian Conococheague Formation, but some maps also show it as the Cambrian

Buffalo Springs limestone. This is a very limited locality in size, but it offers the opportunity to see stromatolites in Cambrian carbonates. Stromatolites are best described as fossil algae, and they formed as layers and layers of algae grew and were flattened during the formation of the associated limestones. The brownish ribbed features observed in the rocks at this site are the fossilized stromatolites. The site also has some bedded limestones in outcrop, which can make interesting display pieces if you find a good piece. The site is also reported to have trilobites, but despite my efforts, I was unable to find any fossil-bearing zones. My experience in Pennsylvania is that fossils are extremely hard to find in Cambrian rocks, so I was not too surprised when I could not find any trilobites at this outcrop. If you collect at this site, be very careful about the traffic, as it is very heavy on this road. The site is not posted but still is private ground, so be aware that access to these roadside outcrops can change at any time.

Reference: Busch and Fedosh, 1978

7. Fruitville Pike Pseudomorphs

The pseudomorphs are goethite and limonite after pyrite, and are generally cubes with rounded edges.

County: Lancaster

Site type: Goethite pseudomorphs after pyrite on ground surface

Land status: Manheim Township land, not posted

Material: Cubes and pyritohedrons of goethite after pyrite

Host rock: Soil, material is weathered from Cambrian-age Ledger dolomite

Difficulty: Easy, but getting harder every year

Family-friendly: Yes

Tools needed: Gloves, small pointed hammer or screwdriver

Special concerns: Site has been picked over, collecting gets more difficult every year

Special attractions: Lancaster City, Amish Country attractions

GPS parking: N40° 05' 13" / W76° 19' 19"

GPS field (general area for collecting): N40° 05' 11" / W76° 19' 11"

The pseudomorphs are found in the field and within the tree rows in the background.

Topographic quadrangle: Lancaster, PA
Finding the site: Take US 30 to the Fruitville Pike exit in Lancaster, and turn north on Fruitville Pike. Proceed approximately 1.5 miles to Delp Road and turn right (east). Continue approximately 0.4 mile, turn right (south) on Bassett Drive, make a U-turn, proceed approximately 600 feet, and park on the east side of Bassett Drive so that you are parking on the opposite side of the residential properties along this street. You can then walk to the fields with the pseudomorphs.

Rockhounding:

If you like low-intensity collecting, walking, and looking for interesting minerals on the ground, this is the site for you. The pseudomorphs formed in the Ledger dolomite and have weathered out of the dolomite and been repeatedly turned over by the plowing of the fields. The pseudomorphs lie directly on the ground and are generally cubes with rounded edges. They are found in the plowed fields and in the rows of evergreen trees just east of the plowed fields. This locality also has pyritohedrons, which are twelve-sided crystals with pentagonal crystal faces.

They generally have irregular shapes and not all of the crystal faces have sides of equal length. Many of the larger pseudomorphs are found as fragments. Gloves and a small pointed-tip rock hammer to pry up rocks from the clay soil are useful to protect your hands.

This is a good place to take kids and get them to find pseudomorphs by saying that they are looking for "magic crystals." The more eyes on the ground, the more pseudomorphs you are likely to find. However, this locality has been picked over pretty well. You can still find pseudomorphs, but you can expect that it may take some time to find them. Of course, you may always get lucky and find a large pyritohedron immediately.

References: Beard, 2002; Geyer et al., 1976

Sites 7–15

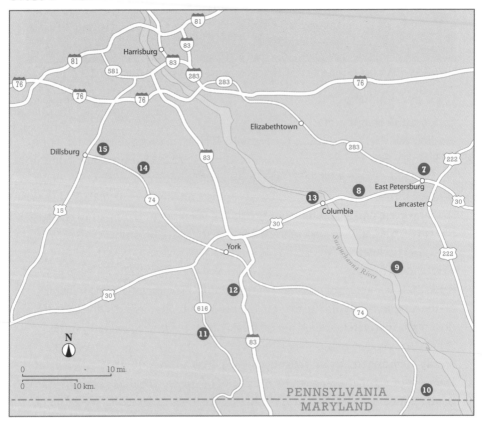

8. Mud and Grubb Lake Goethite Bombshells

Some of the goethite is very hard and glossy. This specimen was caked with mud when first uncovered near Mud Lake.

See map page 44.

County: Lancaster

Site type: Nodules that weather out of mud banks

Land status: West Hempfield Township Park at Grubb Lake; uncertain of status around Mud Lake, uncertain of collecting status at both sites

Material: Masses of goethite and limonite

Host rock: Soil; material is weathered from Cambrian-age Ledger dolomite

Difficulty: Easy

Family-friendly: Yes, but hike to Mud Lake site may be tough and muddy

Tools needed: Hammer, chisel, small shovel, bucket, backpack

Special concerns: Ticks, collecting site can be very muddy, uncertain of land status

Special attractions: Fishing at Grubb Lake

The ravine that leads to the Mud Lake collecting area has many fallen trees, and it can be a tough area for hiking.

GPS parking for Grubb Lake (lots of parking space): N40° 3' 32" / W76° 26' 41"
GPS parking for Mud Lake (very limited parking space): N40° 3' 21" / W76° 27' 2"
GPS main Mud Lake collecting area: N40° 3' 25" / W76° 27' 20"
Topographic quadrangle: Columbia East, PA
Finding the site: To park at the Grubb Lake site, take PA 23 west from Lancaster to the small community of Silver Spring. Just past Silver Spring turn left (south) onto Hempfield Hill Road, and take this south 0.6 mile to the parking lot for Grubb Lake. To park at the trailhead for Mud Lake, continue south from the Grubb Lake parking area approximately 0.3 mile to Vista Road, turn right (west), and proceed approximately 0.3 mile. Vista Road will turn into Sycamore Drive. Park at the small opening near Mud Lake on the left (west) side of the road. You can then hike to the Mud Lake collecting area from here.

Rockhounding

This is actually two field trips that can be done either together or separately, depending on the group you are with. The Grubb Lake site basically requires a walk around the lake, and you can find some goethite and limonite fragments in the washes on the west side of the lake. For collectors, the Mud Lake site is by far the better of the two sites, but it can be more work to access—you will get very muddy if you do any serious collecting at this area. The first time I came here I had to hike overland to get to Mud Lake. It was a terrible hike as I had to cross many large sections of briars and muddy slopes. However, when I found the collecting area, it was worth the effort. I later found the trail to get to the Mud Lake collecting area, and this is reached via the small parking area for Mud Lake. You can find very large masses of goethite, and many of these are very glossy black and make excellent display pieces. Some of the goethite also forms as hollow shells, and these are often referred to as bombshells as they resemble fragments of exploded cannon balls. A hammer, chisel, and a small shovel are useful for the collecting area at Mud Lake, but any collecting around Grubb Lake is likely to be limited to loose rocks in some of the drainages around the lake. I highly recommend bringing a bucket as the specimens are very muddy. A backpack is also helpful as you will want to carry your tools to the site due to its significant distance from the car.

References: Geyer et al., 1976; Meisler and Becher, 1971

9. Safe Harbor Quarry

This rock is a dark purple-gray hornfels with some waxy minerals that may be antigorite.

See map page 44.
County: Lancaster
Site type: Former quarry
Land status: Safe Harbor Water Power Corporation, public access
Material: Contact metamorphic minerals
Host rock: Cambrian rocks intruded by late Triassic/early Jurassic diabase
Difficulty: Difficult
Family-friendly: Yes, scenic hiking, but mineral collecting and identification difficult
Tools needed: Hammer, gloves
Special concerns: Ticks, area is very overgrown, rock piles unstable
Special attractions: Fishing in Susquehanna River and Safe Harbor Dam
GPS parking: N39° 55' 40" / W76° 22' 38"
GPS north end of quarry: N39° 55' 53" / W76° 22' 26"

The southern quarry has a small pond, and the rocks are best exposed on the east side.

GPS south end of quarry: N39° 55' 42" / W76° 22' 32"
Topographic quadrangle: Conestoga and Safe Harbor, PA
Finding the site: From US 30 in Columbia, Pennsylvania, turn south onto PA 441, aka North Third Street. Continue south on PA 441, which becomes Water Street, for approximately 3.8 miles. PA 441 then ends at the junction of PA 999 and becomes River Road. Continue south on River Road for approximately 7.6 miles to the intersection of Power House Road and River Road at Safe Harbor. From this intersection, proceed south on River Road for approximately 0.3 mile and look for a turnoff to the left (north). Park at this turnoff and take the trail that goes into the woods. You will soon come to an old concrete road that heads north. Follow this and stay to the right, and you soon will be at the location for the area between the north quarry and the south quarry. The south quarry has a fairly large shallow pond.

Rockhounding

The Safe Harbor Quarry was developed to extract rock to build the Safe Harbor Dam. The dam was built from 1929 to 1931, and approximately 2,300,000 tons of rocks were extracted from the quarry for construction of the dam. This was a fairly large quarry, but very few signs remain. The only remnants are the concrete road, some reported concrete structures for the former crushing plant, and the void in the hills left by the quarry. It is amazing to consider that this project was begun at the start of the Great Depression and took only two years to complete. Today, such a project would likely never receive the environmental approvals, and even if it could get approved, the permitting and studies themselves would likely take more than ten years.

The quarry exposures received attention from mineralogists in the 1940s and 1950s. The quarry is roughly divided into two halves, which I refer to as the northern and southern quarries. A late Triassic/early Jurassic diabase dike is reported within the northern end of the northern quarry, and contact metamorphic minerals are reported to be in this area. During my visits to the quarry, my finds have been mostly limited to the host rock formations, which are the Cambrian Antietam/Harpers Formations, which are mainly fine-grained schists, and the Cambrian Vintage dolomite, which is a fine-grained gray dolomite. I have found some hornfelsic rocks with waxy serpentine-like minerals, which I assume are antigorite, and some minor rocks with dark mica, which is either biotite or phlogopite, and pegmatitic zones that are mainly light-tan feldspar and quartz. Dravite, which is a magnesium-bearing brown tourmaline, is reportedly present in the Safe Harbor Quarry, but it is also reported to be very hard to find. I verified that it is very difficult to find at this site.

The quarry is very overgrown and the rock piles along the sides are very unstable, and it is a difficult quarry for collecting. I highly recommend strong boots, long pants, long sleeves, gloves, and insect repellent. The best time to collect would be in late fall when the vegetation is least, but the leaves and fallen trees will still obscure many of the rocks. The key to finding minerals at this site is to find the diabase dike and the associated contact zone. Geologic maps of the area show the location within the north end of the quarry, but when I was there I did not see any evidence of the contact zone. Most of the rocks that I found were relatively unaltered schists and carbonates.

Although it is difficult to find minerals at this site, it is a quarry that you can access, and you are likely to have considerable solitude. Although the area has public access, I am uncertain if mineral collecting is a permitted use, but I also did not see any signs specifically prohibiting mineral collecting. After your visit to the quarry, be sure to stop by the Safe Harbor Dam site for a good view of the Susquehanna River and some fishing. You may also want to look at some of the riprap along the side of the river. Much of this is limestone and some of it has very coarse zones with excellent cleavage and large white crystals.

References: Blackmer, 2007; Chapman, 1950; Smith, 1978; Thomlinson, 1942

10. Delta Slate Quarries

See map page 44.
County: York
Site type: Slate along roadside
Land status: Private, well posted, very limited collecting only outside of posted areas
Material: Dark gray to black slate
Host rock: Peach Bottom slate
Difficulty: Easy
Family-friendly: No, as area is posted against trespassing; no access without permission
Tools needed: None, no collecting allowed
Special concerns: Traffic along road sides, land access
Special attractions: None
GPS parking: N39° 44' 11" / W76° 18' 03"
Topographic quadrangle: Delta, PA-MD
Finding the site: Take PA 74 to the intersection with PA 851, and turn south onto the Delta Bypass, aka Broad Street, and proceed approximately 1.5 miles to the town of Delta. In Delta turn left (east) onto Peach Bottom Road, and follow this 0.7 mile to the intersection with Pikes Peak Road. Peach Bottom Road then becomes Atom Road. Proceed approximately 0.5 mile, and look for the large slate dumps on the south side of the road. A small parking area is located along the road and is marked by some large blocks of slate. The quarry just south of this area is known as the Funkhausers Quarry.

Rockhounding

This is a site that is completely off-limits for access to the quarries, but it is still an interesting site to drive around, and there are small pieces of slate along the side of the road that are outside of the posted signs. The quarries are in the Peach Bottom slate, which was first used in 1734 and quarried until the 1940s. The Funkhauser Quarry is the largest of the quarries—it is approximately 3,000 feet long and about 500 feet wide. The geology of the area is quite complex. The slate is considered to be Ordovician but it is within tightly folded and metamorphosed Precambrian rocks. The slate is interesting in hand specimen as it is very smooth and can be split into relatively thin sheets with a hammer and small chisel.

The piles of slate can be viewed from your car when driving on the adjacent public roads.

The quarries were formerly known as a big party spot, and several people have drowned here. They are reportedly among the most dangerous in the United States for accidental drownings. Unauthorized use has reportedly dropped off since the area is regularly patrolled. If you decide to visit this area, make sure you do not trespass—stay outside of the posted areas.

Reference: Stose and Jonas, 1939

11. Strickhousers Iron Mines

Loose pieces of rock have distinct tiny octahedrons of magnetite.

See map page 44.

County: York

Site type: Former iron mines

Land status: P. Joseph Raab County Park, collecting not allowed

Material: Specular hematite and octahedral magnetite

Host rock: Cambrian-age Harpers phyllite and Antietam quartzite

Difficulty: Easy

Family-friendly: Yes, excellent hiking trails and easy access

Tools needed: None, no collecting allowed

Special concerns: Trail moderately strenuous

Special attractions: Codorus State Park

GPS parking: N39° 50' 54" / W76° 48' 44"

GPS mines: N39° 50' 33" / W76° 48' 55"

(Note that iron mines are on both sides of the creek)

This is one of the larger mines and is on the east side of the creek.

Topographic quadrangle: Seven Valleys, PA
Finding the site: From I-83 north of York, take US 30 5.3 miles west to PA 462, continue 0.5 miles, then turn left (south) on PA 616. Proceed approximately 5.7 miles to Green Valley Road and turn right (west), and follow this 2.1 miles to Hoff Road and turn right (north). The parking area is approximately 3,500 feet north, on the left side of the road.

Rockhounding

This site contains former iron mines that were worked from approximately 1854 to the 1890s by the York Iron Company. The surrounding areas later became farms, while the mines retreated into the woods. In 1993 the area was donated to York County by Modern Landfill and named in honor of York County Parks' "founding father," P. Joseph Raab. The mines are listed on the National Register of Historic Places.

The iron mineralization consists of platy specular hematite and octahedrons of magnetite. The ore appears shiny in loose rocks on the ground and in outcrop, and the octahedral shape of the magnetite is easy to see in the rocks. The entrances to the mines have been sealed with grates to keep people out, but they still allow bats to come in and out of the mines. The mineralization occurs in the Cambrian-age Harpers phyllite and Antietam quartzite and is disseminated throughout the rocks in the mine areas. This is an excellent place to see old mines and unique iron mineralization. However, due to the historic nature of the site, visitors must stay on designated trails, and no rock collecting is allowed at this site.

References: Geyer et al., 1976; Stose and Jonas, 1939

12. Howard Tunnel Phyllite

Shiny phyllite with tiny limonite pseudomorphs after pyrite is easily found outside the west entrance of the Howard Tunnel.

See map page 44.
County: York
Site type: Outcrops adjacent to rail tunnel
Land status: Heritage Rail Trail County Park
Material: Phyllite
Host rock: Cambrian Harpers Formation
Difficulty: Easy
Family-friendly: Yes, excellent place for a short hike
Tools needed: None, no collecting allowed
Special concerns: No collecting allowed, lots of bike traffic
Special attractions: Richard M. Nixon County Park and Lake Redman
GPS parking: N39° 53' 46" / W76° 44' 39"
GPS Howard Tunnel east entrance: N39° 53' 31" / W76° 44' 57"

The Howard Tunnel is the oldest continually operating rail tunnel in the United States.

Howard Tunnel west entrance: N39° 53' 27" / W76° 45' 00"
Topographic quadrangles: York and West York, PA
Finding the site: From I-83, take exit 14 west to Leader Heights Road, which is also PA 182. Continue west approximately 0.5 mile, turn south on South George Street, proceed about 270 feet, and take the immediate right (west) onto Reynolds Mill Road. Continue on Reynolds Mill Road for approximately 2 miles past Leader

Heights, and turn right (north) onto Twin Arch Road. Proceed about 0.1 mile, and pull over to the right (east) side of Twin Arch Road and park. You can walk to the rail trail and the Howard Tunnel from here.

Rockhounding

This site offers the opportunity to hike through a rail tunnel and observe some shiny phyllite with tiny limonite pseudomorphs of former pyrite crystals. The phyllite is best seen outside of the west tunnel entrance. No collecting or hammering is allowed, but it is easy to view the outcrops up close and observe lots of loose phyllite on the ground outside entrances to the tunnel.

The Howard Tunnel is part of the Heritage Rail Trail County Park. Unlike most rail trails, the rail line adjacent to the trail is still active and is reportedly the oldest continually operating rail line in the United States. The tunnel was built in the late 1830s and was expanded to double rail lines in the 1870s. This later posed problems when larger freight cars went through the tunnel, as they had to be tilted with jacks so they would not hit the lower parts of the arches. The railroad was later converted to a single line, eliminating the freight-car problem, but by then the cargo market had moved to bigger and better railroads along the Susquehanna River and elsewhere.

On a sad historical note, the tunnel has seen three presidential funeral processions. The bodies of Presidents Lincoln, McKinley, and Harding all passed through the Howard Tunnel. Richard M. Nixon County Park, named for the thirty-seventh president, is also nearby, so the area has a unique connection to presidential as well as geologic history.

References: Gunnarsson, 1991; Stose and Jonas, 1939

13. Accomac Road Serpentine Minerals

The outcrops are on the east side of Accomac Road near the Susquehanna River.

See map page 44.
County: York
Site type: Road outcrops and float at drainage outlet into river
Land status: Private, not posted, may be along highway right-of-way
Material: Serpentine minerals
Host rock: Precambrian-age metabasalt
Difficulty: Easy
Family-friendly: Yes, but best collecting is next to river
Tools needed: Hammer
Special concerns: Traffic along Accomac Road
Special attractions: Susquehanna River
GPS parking: N40° 02' 40" / W76° 33' 47"
Topographic quadrangle: Columbia West, PA

Some fibrous minerals can be seen in this hand sample of rock found in the drainage area near Accomac Road.

Finding the site: From US 30, take the exit for Cool Springs Road and head north approximately 0.4 mile to Dark Hollow Road. Turn left (west) on Dark Hollow Road, and proceed 0.9 mile to Accomac Road. Turn north (right) onto Accomac Road, and continue 0.4 mile to River Road, which roughly parallels the Susquehanna River. Just before you reach River Road you will pass the metabasalt with serpentine outcrops on the right (east) side of Accomac Road. Park at the parking area near the river, across from the Accomac Inn, and walk back to the outcrops. Just to the west of the parking area is a drainage channel to the Susquehanna River with abundant metabasalt and serpentine rocks.

Rockhounding

These outcrops are within a mass of metabasalt that has been partially serpentinized. Most of the rocks that I saw in this area are dark-green metabasalt with minor serpentine minerals. However, in the rocks within the drainage, I found several rocks with various shades of green, and cracking open some of these rocks revealed fibrous sections and other green serpentine minerals.

Reference: Stose and Jonas, 1939

14. Rossville Malachite-Azurite

The azurite and malachite can be seen inside of the workings, but visitors to the site should stay outside as the workings are too dangerous to enter.

See map page 44.
County: York
Site type: Small workings in roadcut
Land status: Private, likely highway right-of-way
Material: Malachite and azurite
Host rock: Dark gray hornfels
Difficulty: Easy
Family-friendly: Yes, but must be careful of traffic; well worth a stop
Tools needed: Hammer
Special concerns: Opening is not safe to enter, traffic on highway, site is very picked over and visitors should limit what they collect
Special attractions: Gifford Pinchot State Park

The roadcut is relatively east to spot from Highway 74.

GPS parking: N40° 04' 19" / W76° 55' 26"

Topographic quadrangle: Wellsville, PA

Finding the site: From I-83, take exit 35 and head west on PA 177 toward Gifford Pinchot State Park. Continue on PA 177 approximately 9.1 miles to Rossville, and turn north on PA 74 in Rossville. Continue north for approximately 0.7 mile, look to the right (east) for small workings on the side of the road, and pull over at the workings. The road is quite wide in this area and there is enough space for more than one car if needed.

Rockhounding

This is a unique site in that it is very accessible, near a state park (which offers other recreational activities), and the copper mineralization includes azurite as well as malachite. The mineralization resulted from hydrothermal activity from nearby Triassic diabases that intruded shales of the Triassic Gettysburg Formation. The shales were then "baked" into hornfels, which is a contact metamorphic rock formed from the intrusion of igneous rocks into fine-grained, noncalcareous sediments. The mineralization was discovered when the road was widened in the early 1970s. The site has been picked over by thousands of rock hounds, but it still yields small pieces of malachite and azurite, although they get smaller and smaller every year. Collectors should limit their collecting at this site. The workings have become wider and deeper over the years as well, and I recommend that you stay out of them and confine any collecting to the rocks outside of the workings. Interestingly, this mineralization is localized, and I have not found any other outcrops along the roadcut that have any visible traces of copper mineralization.

References: Hoskins et al., 1976; Smith and O'Neill, 1973

15. Dillsburg Diabase Minerals

The vein in this diabase was very light green and typical of the mineralization at this locality.

See map page 44.
County: York
Site type: Outcrops and hill slope along highway
Land status: Private, not posted, sections may be in highway right-of-way
Material: Vein minerals in diabase
Host rock: Triassic diabase
Difficulty: Easy
Family-friendly: Yes
Tools needed: Hammer
Special concerns: Private land, not currently posted but can change at any time
Special attractions: Williams Grove Flea Market on Sundays
GPS parking: N40° 07' 06" / W76° 02' 11"
Topographic quadrangle: Dillsburg, PA

Finding the site: Take US 15 to the southern intersection with PA 74, which is North Baltimore Street in Dillsburg. Do not confuse this road with the northern intersection with PA 74, which is York Road. At the time of this writing in 2012, there was a large closed car dealership on the east side of US 15 just north of the southern intersection with PA 74, and it was possible to park on the north side of this lot. This parking area is only about 500 feet north of the intersection of North Baltimore Street and US 15. The diabase area is immediately north of the lot. If this dealership reopens or another business occupies this parking location, find a parking space on a side road off of North Baltimore Street, park, and walk to the diabase from there.

Rockhounding

This area is a broad, slightly sloping hillside of Triassic diabase. The hillside appears to have been graded, and this has exposed the diabase and broken many of the rocks on the surface. The area is basically a large slope of diabase rubble. Zeolite minerals, including laumontite, leonhardite, apophyllite, and natrolite have been reported in a diabase roadcut, approximately 1.5 miles south on US 15, but this roadcut is too dangerous for access, and the adjoining properties are clearly posted against trespassing. However, given the geographic proximity of the diabase just north of PA 74 with the diabase roadcut to the south, it seems reasonable that the mineralogy should be similar, as they are both mapped as Triassic diabase by the Pennsylvania Geological Survey.

Walking through the diabase just north of PA 74 reveals some minor vein material in the diabase. Much of this is light green, and I have assumed this is prehnite, but prehnite was not reported in the diabase to the south. However, the zeolite mineral apophyllite is reported to be present to the south, so perhaps this is light-green apophyllite. Some of the vein material is also calcareous and presumably calcite, as it effervesces with dilute hydrochloric acid. A good hammer is a necessity at this locality, as you must break open the rocks to determine if you have found a good mineralized zone. Most of the diabase is solid and barren of minerals, but the zones with potential minerals are very easy to spot as they are generally white or light green, and this contrasts well against the dark-green to dark-gray color of the diabase.

References: Lapham, 1963; Lapham and Geyer, 1969

16. Hershey Specular Hematite

The specular hematite occurs on the surface of the rocks as aggregates of crystal blades.

County: Dauphin
Site type: Small borrow pits with specular hematite and occasionally garnet
Land status: Private but not posted
Material: Specular hematite and small garnets
Host rock: Triassic-age siltstones of the Gettysburg Formation
Difficulty: Easy
Family-friendly: Yes, but be careful when crossing Bullfrog Valley Road
Tools needed: Hammer, small shovel, bucket
Special concerns: May encounter ticks, centipedes, insects in leaves and soil; land status
Special attractions: Bullfrog Valley Park, Hershey Park
GPS parking: N40° 15' 26" / W76° 41' 02"
GPS trailhead: N40° 15' 23" / W76° 40' 57"
Topographic quadrangle: Middletown, PA

The former iron mining pits are overgrown with trees, but you can find hematite in loose rocks on the ground.

Finding the site: From US 322 on the west side of Hershey, turn south onto Bullfrog Valley Road, which is just west of the Hershey Medical Center. Continue south on Bullfrog Valley Road approximately 0.8 mile to Bullfrog Valley Park, which is on the west side of the road. Park in the parking lot and walk approximately 300 feet south along Bullfrog Valley Road. Cross the road to a small asphalt drainage channel on the east side of the road. Follow this drainage up the hill to a path that leads into the woods. Small prospect pits, which are well hidden by leaves and trees, are on both the sides of the path.

Rockhounding

Specular hematite and tiny red garnets are found in siltstones that have been contact-metamorphosed by nearby diabase intrusions. This is a very old iron-mining area, and the former pits are very indistinct and well overgrown. Look for shiny specular hematite in rocks near the pits and in loose pieces on the ground. If you find a location with loose rocks, you may find additional hematite by digging out the rocks and opening them with your hammer. The garnets are very small but often well crystallized and can be seen well with a hand lens. I have found most of the garnet-bearing rocks by digging loose rocks out of the north side of the path along the trail entrance next to Bullfrog Valley Road.

References: Beard, 2006; Lapham et al., 1969

Sites 16–18

17. Fontana Quarries Calcite

Tan and white calcite with well-defined cleavage is easily found on the waste rock pile.

See map page 68.
County: Lebanon
Site type: Waste rock outside of quarry
Land status: Private but not posted
Material: White and tan calcite, banded limestone
Host rock: Cambrian Buffalo Springs Limestone
Difficulty: Easy
Family-friendly: Yes, but stay next to road and outside of posted ground
Tools needed: Hammer
Special concerns: Private land, access may change at any time
Special attractions: Hershey Park
GPS parking: N40° 16' 05" / W76° 28' 50"
Topographic quadrangle: Lebanon, PA
Finding the site: Take US 322 to PA 241, also known as Mt. Wilson Road, and turn south. Continue on 241 south for approximately 1 mile, and as the road turns to

The pile is fairly large and adjacent to the road.

the west, take the first left to the south, which is Road T-404. In approximately 600 feet the road will fork. Take the fork to the left, and proceed toward the quarry gate. The large piles of limestone waste rock are on the north side of the road just a few hundred feet west of the outside of the gate. Do not proceed past the locked quarry gate.

Rockhounding

Quarries are excellent collecting locations but nearly all of them are off-limits to casual collectors. Active quarries often require significant advance planning and are best visited by groups, and inactive quarries are generally clearly posted against trespassing. However, it is often worthwhile to check near the edges of quarries to see if any rock piles or outcrops are adjacent to the operation.

The Fontana Quarry is currently inactive and the main access roads are locked and clearly posted against trespassing. However, there is a significant large pile of waste rock adjacent to the road, and at the time of my visit in May 2012, it was not posted, and it was easy to exit my vehicle and look at these rocks. White and tan massive calcite is easily found, and much of the limestone on the large pile is conspicuously banded. Pyrite, garnet, and selenite are also reported from the quarry, but I was unable to find any of these on this waste rock pile.

References: Geyer et al., 1958; Geyer et al., 1976

18. Cornwall Magnetite

The magnetite outcrops are prominent on the bottom of the southern edge of the Big Hill.

See map page 68.
County: Lebanon
Site type: Mine tailings and outcrops
Land status: Private but not posted
Material: Magnetite in outcrops and colorful rocks in mine tailings
Host rock: Contact-metamorphosed conglomerates, shales, and limestones of the Ordovician-age Hamburg Sequence
Difficulty: Easy
Family-friendly: Yes, but limited parking and must be careful when walking on and adjacent to the tailings pile
Tools needed: Hammer, chisel
Special concerns: Limited parking, potential access issues, easy to pinch fingers and trip on mine tailings rocks
Special attractions: Cornwall Iron Furnace

The Big Hill is a large tailings pile, and many colorful rocks can be found on its slopes.

GPS parking: N40° 16' 8" / W76° 24' 18"
GPS magnetite outcrop: N40° 16' 7" / W76° 24' 14"
Topographic quadrangle: Lebanon, PA
Finding the site: Take US 322 to the PA 117 exit, and take PA 117, aka Ironmaster Road, east 0.9 mile to the intersection with Burd Coleman Road. Turn left (north) on Burd Coleman Road, proceed 0.5 mile, and then right (east) onto Rexmont Road, and continue 0.5 mile. This road will curve to the north. Turn right (south) onto Boyd Street, and follow this approximately 0.3 mile to the parking area, which is on the east side of Boyd Street and directly opposite the large reservoir of the former Cornwall iron-mine open pit. Parking is extremely limited and is best for a single car. From the parking area, a trail leads directly to the tailings of the "Big Hill," and the magnetite outcrops are on the flanks of the south side of the slope.

Rockhounding

The Cornwall Iron Mines were the largest deposit of iron ore in the eastern United States, and at one time the main workings were the largest open-pit mine in the world. The main open-pit workings closed for good when they were flooded during Hurricane Agnes in 1972, and these workings are now a large water reservoir. The former open pit and reservoir are fenced and not accessible, but a large section of the former workings are just east of the reservoir. This area is known as the Big Hill, a large slope that is covered with large rocks from the mine workings. Most of these rocks are metamorphosed sediments. The "blue conglomerate" rocks in these tailings are dark gray and often spotted with orange feldspar crystals, and many other colorful rocks can be found in tailings. The southern side of the Big Hill has outcrops of metamorphosed sediments with coarse grains of magnetite, and these are easily identified as they are attracted to a magnet. This outcrop is an excellent source of magnetite for schoolkids or other groups that would like to see magnetic rocks. Although the area is not posted and is undoubtedly visited by rock hounds and others, be aware that access may change at any time.

References: Geyer et al., 1958; Geyer et al., 1976; Lapham and Gray, 1972

19. Antietam Molybdenite

The molybdenite occurs as small metallic flakes in the hornblende gneiss host rock.

County: Berks
Site type: Cliff along roadside
Land status: Private, likely in highway right-of-way
Material: Molybdenite
Host rock: Hornblende gneiss
Difficulty: Difficult
Family-friendly: No, as the molybdenite is very hard to see. This site is best for advanced collectors.
Tools needed: Hammer, chisel, hand lens
Special concerns: Traffic on road
Special attractions: Reading Pagoda, Antietam Reservoir
GPS parking: N40° 21' 33" / W75° 52' 10"
GPS molybdenite in outcrop: N40° 21' 16" / W75° 52' 11"
Topographic quadrangle: Birdsboro, PA
Finding the site: Take US 422 to Mount Penn, where US 422 turns into Perkiomen Avenue. Turn north on Carsonia Avenue, and follow Carsonia Avenue 1.9 miles northeast until it intersects with Antietam Road. Turn left on Antietam Road, and

The molybdenite bearing outcrops appear to be limited to the area just southeast of the dam on the east side of Antietam Road. Once you cross the road the area is reasonably safe for observing the outcrops.

follow this northeast for approximately 0.5 mile until you see Antietam Reservoir on the west side of Antietam Road. Angora Road intersects Antietam Road and goes around the reservoir, but stay on Antietam Road. Park on the west side of Antietam Road at one of the parking areas used to access trails to the reservoir. The best parking area is just northeast of the reservoir. The outcrops with the molybdenite are in the cliffs on the east side of Antietam Road.

Rockhounding

This locality has cliff outcrops of hornblende gneiss that has minor grains of disseminated molybdenite, which is molybdenum sulfide (MoS_2). The molybdenite occurs as silvery-gray platy flecks in the gneiss. The gneiss is dark gray and rich in plagioclase feldspar. The rocks in the cliffs are extremely hard and it is difficult to break off pieces for hand specimens. Powellite, which is a rare calcium molybdate ($CaMoS_2$) is also reported at this locality, and it can be identified in hand specimens as it has an adamantine luster and is fluorescent under ultraviolet light.

My experience at this site has indicated that the molybdenite is concentrated in one area of the cliffs, directly across from where Angora Road intersects Antietam Road. You have to get up close to the cliffs and look carefully for the silvery-gray flecks of molybdenite. I have not been able to find powellite at this site, but this would be an excellent site to check at night with a portable ultraviolet light to look for fluorescent powellite.

References: MacLachlan, 1992; Pierotti et al., 2006; Smith, 1975

Sites 19–22

20. Allentown Jasper Cliffs

The jasper is generally orange and brown, and this piece also has some red jasper.

See map page 77.
County: Lehigh
Site type: Outcrops and loose rocks on hillside
Land status: South Mountain Park
Material: Orange, brown, and red jasper
Host rock: Conglomerate of the Cambrian-age Hardyston Formation
Difficulty: Easy
Family-friendly: Yes
Tools needed: None, likely no collecting allowed
Special concerns: Land status for collecting uncertain. No clearly posted restrictions, but rock collecting is almost certainly not allowed.
Special attractions: Dorney Park in Allentown for kids, Sands Casino in Bethlehem for adults
GPS parking: N40° 33' 53" / W75° 27' 47"
GPS Jasper Cliffs: N40° 33' 51" / W75° 27' 47"

The best jasper is below the base of the cliffs and often occurs in large piles around trees.

Topographic quadrangle: Allentown West, PA
Finding the site: From I-78, take exit 57 and turn north onto West Emaus Avenue. Proceed approximately 0.8 mile and turn right onto South 10th Street. Continue southeast on South 10th Street for approximately 0.4 mile to South Mountain Park, and follow the road to its highest point, which is just northwest of the Jasper Cliffs.

Rockhounding

The Jasper Cliffs are not really jasper but conglomerate of the Cambrian-age Hardyston Formation with minor jasper. The cliffs are just southeast of the road and can be reached by walking up trails from the road. The jasper is generally orange and brown, and occasionally red. Vein quartz is present in some of the rocks, which form interesting white patterns against the yellow, brown, and red of the jasper. Much of the jasper lies in large piles below the base of the cliffs, and there are many large areas that appear to be former pits to extract the jasper. The cliffs themselves are mainly conglomerate of the Hardyston Formation and do not appear to have as much jasper as the areas toward the bottom of the cliffs. The area is heavily overgrown and you have to be careful of briars and loose rocks. While collecting is almost certainly not allowed due to its status as a park, the area is well worth visiting and reviewing from a geologic standpoint, as this type of jasper occurrence does not occur outside of this region in Pennsylvania.

Reference: Geyer and Bolles, 1979

21. Constitution Drive Rare Earth Minerals

Allanite crystals can be found in the boulders of the upper pegmatite quarry.

See map page 77.
County: Lehigh
Site type: Former quarries on roadside
Land status: Lehigh Uplands Preserve, no posted restrictions on access
Material: Allanite, thorite, zircon, orange orthoclase/microcline
Host rock: Precambrian Byram gneiss and Cambrian Hardyston Formation
Difficulty: Easy to moderately difficult
Family-friendly: Yes, but somewhat remote road
Tools needed: Hammer, chisel
Special concerns: Land status for collecting uncertain, road is reportedly haunted
Special attractions: Dorney Park in Allentown for kids, Sands Casino in Bethlehem for adults
GPS lower pegmatite quarry: N40° 36' 00" / W75° 26' 20"

GPS upper pegmatite quarry: N40° 35' 58" / W75° 26' 20"
GPS lower conglomerate quarry: N40° 36' 2" / W75° 26' 14"
Topographic quadrangle: Allentown East, PA
Finding the site: From I-78, take PA 145 north approximately 2.2 miles to East Susquehanna Street, which is on the southeast side of Allentown and south of the Lehigh River. Turn right (east) on East Suquehanna Street, and proceed approximately 0.5 mile to Constitution. Turn left (north) onto Constitution Drive, which goes through a dense area of row houses and then bends eastward. Constitution Drive soon becomes a partially unpaved, relatively rough road. Proceed to the stone monument on the right side of the road, which marks the boundary between Allentown and Salisbury townships. This monunment is approximately 1 mile from the intersection of Constitution Drive and East Susquehanna Street; it is an important landmark for orienting yourself at this site. Approximately 665 feet east of the monument is a spring, which is easy to see as it is a large bricked wall on the south side of the road, and this is also an important reference point for your location. The first quarry, which is mainly granitic pegmatite, is 210 feet east of this spring. Proceed another 420 feet and you will see a small trail that proceeds to another pegmatite quarry up the hill and to the south, which is the Upper Pegmatite Quarry. Another quarry, which is within conglomerate, is 1,200 feet east of the spring and is referred to as the Lower Conglomerate Quarry. The spring and the township boundary are by far the best reference points in the area.

Rockhounding

These quarries are heavily overgrown and it is not immediately apparent that they are former quarries. The granitic pegmatite quarry is mainly coarse-grained granitic Byram gneiss with some minor zones of pegmatites, but the pegmatitic areas do not have any significantly sized crystals. The upper pegmatite quarry has some excellent examples of allanite crystals and coarse-grained granite. The lower conglomerate quarry is within the base of the Cambrian-age Hardyston Formation, and some good examples of metaconglomerate can be found in this quarry. The lower conglomerate quarry also has pinite, which is a fine-grained, dark-gray to black micaceous rock. The pegmatitic rocks and the conglomerate are easy to identify, and the allanite crystals in the upper pegmatite can be found among the boulders in this quarry. The rocks are reportedly enriched in thorium (Th) and some of the rare-earth elements, which include yttrium (Y), rubidium (Rb), lanthanum (La), promethium (Pm), and niobium (Nb).

The Upper Pegmatite Quarry is heavily overgrown and difficult to distinguish as a former quarry.

Several websites say Constitution Drive is haunted by the ghost of a man who was killed by a train while walking his dogs. I knew nothing about this incident when I first visited the site, but I had a very creepy feeling on this road. When I mentioned to my kids that the road was haunted, they both wanted to come to the site, even though they normally never go rockhounding with me. This may be an alternative way to get your kids to come rockhounding, as saying the road is haunted apparently makes it much more interesting to them than saying it is a unique rare-earth mineral locality.

Reference: Geyer et al., 1976

22. Hellertown Thomas Iron Slag

Some of the slag has interesting spherical structures in the partially processed iron ore.

See map page 77.
County: Northampton
Site type: Former ironworks
Land status: Water Street Park, no posted restrictions on access
Material: Iron slag
Host rock: No host rock, slag is only material at this site
Difficulty: Easy
Family-friendly: Yes
Tools needed: Hammer
Special concerns: Land status for collecting uncertain
Special attractions: Lost River Caverns in Hellertown
GPS parking: N40° 34' 49" / W75° 20' 39"
GPS former ironworks: N40° 35' 8" / W75° 20' 46"
Topographic quadrangle: Hellertown, PA
Finding the site: From I-78, take PA 412 approximately 1.4 miles south to West Water Street in Hellertown and turn right (west). Within about 1,000 feet you will

The site is covered with millions of tons of gray iron slag.

see a large parking area on the right (north), which is Water Street Park. Park here and walk north on the former rail line, which has been converted to a trail. Walk left when the road forks. This will take you directly to the former ironworks.

Rockhounding

The Thomas Iron Site is the site of a former ironworks for the Thomas Iron Company, which was headquartered in nearby Hokendauqua, Pennsylvania. The Thomas Iron Site is the former location of Furnaces No. 10 and No. 11. The furnaces were acquired from the Saucon Iron Company by the Thomas Iron Company in 1884. The furnaces were shut down around 1922, and the buildings were removed shortly afterward, but the slag from the furnaces remains. The area is covered by millions of tons of slag. Normally I would never collect slag, but the slag at this site has a wide variety of textures, and while most of it is gray, it does have areas with variation in color. Some of the slag resembles scoria, some is glassy, and some has a ropey appearance. Many slaggy pieces of partially processed iron have tiny globules of iron in a slag matrix. The pieces of partially processed iron ore are red, brown, gray, and black and very hard to break with a hammer. Trying to hammer open these iron-rich pieces is like trying to break apart a piece of steel. Many of the nonoxidized iron-rich pieces are also strongly magnetic. This is a good place for anyone with an interest in the early iron industry in Pennsylvania, and especially for anyone that wants to see millions of tons of slag.

Reference: Bartholomew and Metz, 1988

23. Easton Tremolite and Phologopite

The tremolite is white and fibrous, and bright white pieces can be broken off the boulders in the former quarry.

County: Northampton

Site type: Former quarry on roadside

Land status: Private but not posted

Material: Fibrous and massive white tremolite and platy green phlogopite

Host rock: Precambrian metamorphic rocks

Difficulty: Easy, but there's thick brush and you have to cross a busy highway

Family-friendly: No, brush very thick, ticks, traffic a concern, no guarantee of site access

Tools needed: Hammer, chisel, large sledgehammer if you want to break apart large rocks

Special concerns: Traffic when crossing PA 611, ticks, briars

Special attractions: Crayola Factory, Delaware River

The former quarry is heavily overgrown but you can easily find tremolite and phologopite in loose rocks and in outcrop.

GPS parking: N40° 42' 59" / W75° 11' 36"
GPS quarry: N40° 42' 55" / W75° 11' 42"
Topographic quadrangle: Easton, PA-NJ
Finding the site: Take PA 611 from Easton and proceed north approximately 1.3 miles. A water-filtration plant is on the east side of 611, next to the Delaware River, and this is a useful landmark for approaching the site. You will then pass the former quarry, which is on the west side of 611. The former quarry is difficult to spot as it is heavily overgrown with trees and brush. There is a small parking area in a wide area of the shoulder just north of the water filtration plant. Park here and walk across PA 611 to the quarry, and be extremely careful when crossing the road. Be very careful not to park in any posted areas or in areas that may be too close to the road.

Rockhounding

This is a former quarry with excellent pieces of white tremolite that has both fibrous and massive zones. It is often referred to as the C. K. Williams quarry. Many of the rocks also have platy green phlogopite, which has been called "eastonite." The quarry is quite overgrown, and the best access is generally during winter, as long as there is no snow. Many of the boulders on the ground have some of the best zones for collecting rocks, but you can also find interesting pieces in outcrops along the highwalls. I highly recommend a good rock hammer, and you may even want to consider a large sledgehammer if you want break apart the very large boulders in this former quarry.

References: Geyer et al., 1976; Stepanski and Snow, 2000

Sites 23–25

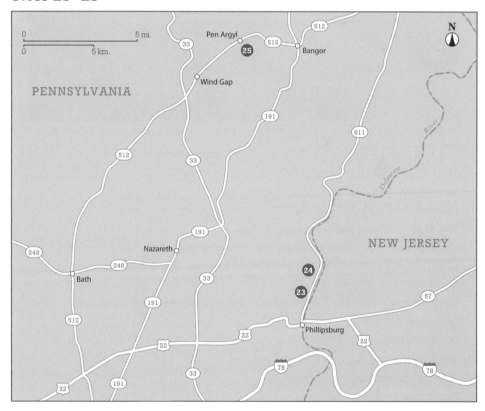

24. St. Anthony's Nose Schorl

Loose pieces with schorl can be found near boulders between the Delaware River and Highway 611 below St. Anthony's Nose.

See map page 87.
County: Northampton
Site type: Boulders along Delaware River
Land status: Northampton County Parks along river, Gollub Park–Forks Township at St. Anthony's Nose Overlook
Material: Black schorl
Host rock: Precambrian granitic gneiss and pegmatites
Difficulty: Easy
Family-friendly: Yes, scenic area, easy access
Tools needed: None, collecting not allowed
Special concerns: Delaware River, must be very careful along river edge, boulders may also be slippery. Overlook is very steep and may not be suitable for smaller children.

Special attractions: Fishing in Delaware River
GPS parking (river): N40° 43' 28" / W75° 11' 17"
GPS parking (trailhead): N40° 43' 04" / W75° 11' 51"
GPS overlook: N40° 43' 21" / W75° 11' 18"
Topographic quadrangle: Easton, PA-NJ
Finding the site: This is actually two sites. The first is along the Delaware River, and the second is an overlook over the Delaware River and into New Jersey. The first site, which offers the opportunity to see schorl in large boulders along the Delaware River, is reached by taking PA 611 north from Easton. Park at the Frost Hollow Overlook, which is a parking area on the east side of the highway approximately 2.3 miles north of the intersection of PA 611 and Bushkill Drive. You can then walk down to the river, go downstream, and look for schorl in the boulders between the riverbank and highway.

The second site is the St. Anthony's Nose overlook. This is reached from US 22 by taking the exit for 13th Street north proceeding about 0.3 mile, and turning right (east) onto West Lafayette Street. Continue on West Lafayette Street for approximately 1.1 miles, turn north on McCartney Street, proceed 300 feet, then left onto Knox Avenue for about 400 feet, and then take the fork to the right to Sullivan Trail. Continue northwest for 0.3 mile on Sullivan Trail, and take a very sharp right (northeast) onto Paxinosa Road East. Continue on this road for approximately 1.1 miles until you reach a small parking area on the left side of the road. You can park and then walk from here, as public vehicles are not allowed on Paxinosa Road past this parking area. Walk on the rest of Paxinosa Road to the east, and you will soon reach a trail that will take you to St. Anthony's Nose overlook.

Rockhounding

Schorl is black, iron-bearing tourmaline. Tourmaline is a complex cyclosilicate of boron and aluminum and typically forms during the latest stages of crystallization in highly siliceous intrusive rocks. Schorl is the most common type of tourmaline, and it is a relatively common mineral in granite pegmatites.

Schorl is reported to occur in the Precambrian gneisses in the roadcut along PA 611 below St. Anthony's Nose. However, you would have to have a serious death wish to want to collect at this roadcut, as the traffic is very heavy and there is no access for collecting, at least from what I could tell by driving through this area. When faced with a locality like this, the best strategy is to look downhill. Sure enough, downhill from St. Anthony's Nose numerous gneissic boulders with coarse pegmatitic zones are common between the river and the highway, and you can

St. Anthony's Nose offers a spectacular outlook over the Delaware River and into New Jersey.

easily access this area and find lots of pieces of rock with schorl. The schorl tends to occur as stubby black crystals and does not have the radiating pattern or elongated crystals that are characteristic of some other black tourmaline occurrences.

The schorl locality along the river is part of the Northampton County Parks system, and rock collecting is apparently not allowed. The river also has many interesting rocks to view, and several large, bright-white pieces of fibrous tremolite can easily be seen in the small, broad peninsula of rocks that extend into the Delaware River.

The overlook at Gollub Park offers an excellent opportunity to get a regional view of the area. However, rock collecting is not permitted in this area either. It is also worth noting that I did not observe any indications of hammering or collecting along the trail in Gollub Park. This overlook site is for looking only, so leave your hammer in the car.

References: Geyer et al., 1976; Smith, 1978

25. Pen Argyl Ordovician Slate

Large pieces of slate can easily be seen on this pile.

See map page 87.
County: Northampton
Site type: Waste rock piles and outcrops
Land status: Private but not posted in some areas; some areas may be municipal property
Material: Slate
Host rock: Pen Argyl slate member of the Ordovician Martinsburg Formation
Difficulty: Easy
Family-friendly: Yes, very limited hiking, slate easily found
Tools needed: Hammer, chisel, flat-bladed screwdriver
Special concerns: Land access uncertain, stay out of posted areas
Special attractions: None
GPS parking: N40° 43' 04" / W75° 11' 51"

Topographic quadrangles: Wind Gap and Bangor, PA

Finding the site: Take PA 512 into Pen Argyl and turn south onto South Main Street. You will immediately see a large parking area to the right (west), and Weona Park is to the left (east). The parking area entrance is only about 250 feet south of the intersection of PA 512 and South Main Street. Turn into the parking area to the west and head about 0.2 mile to the southern end of this large lot. A large slate pile is present at the southern end of the parking area, and the slopes off the southern end also have abundant slate. This area is not fenced or posted against trespassing, but the adjoining quarries are fenced.

Rockhounding

Pen Argyl and the nearby town of Bangor were major producers of slate, and some of the quarries are still active, although production has been greatly scaled back. Slate is all around Pen Argyl, but virtually all of the quarries are fenced and inaccessible. The key is to find areas with slate in ground that is not fenced and not posted against trespassing. This site was an open area during a site visit in April 2012. There are undoubtedly other areas in the region and in Bangor as well, but this site in Pen Argyl offered easy and safe access to see some slate.

The slate is an interesting rock, as it can be split into large, hard pieces with a hammer and bladed chisel, and kids also like to draw on the slate. If you get some good, flat pieces, you can probably occupy some of your kids and their friends for hours with some slate and colored chalk. Larger pieces can also be trimmed and used for garden stepping stones and other uses. The slate is not terribly durable, so it is not good for areas with high foot traffic.

Although this area is not fenced or posted, it also does not have a sign offering free slate. If you visit the area and decide to collect any slate, use discretion and do not leave any large broken pieces, holes, or other issues that may cause the owners to restrict access to this area.

Reference: Drake and Epstein, 1967

26. Saylorsburg Devonian Fossils

The fossiliferous zones are easy to identify as they have voids and "worm holes" that indicate the presence of fossils.

County: Monroe

Site type: Outcrops in roadcut

Land status: Private but not posted, along roadside

Material: Devonian fossils

Host rock: Shales and siltstones of the Devonian-age Mahantango Formation

Difficulty: Easy to moderate

Family-friendly: No, must climb on outcrops, land status a potential issue

Tools needed: Hammer, chisel, flat-bladed screwdriver

Special concerns: Traffic, land status for collecting

Special attractions: Pocono Mountains, various tourist attractions

GPS parking: N40° 54' 4" / W75° 20' 2"

GPS outcrops: N40° 54' 4" / W75° 20' 0"

Topographic quadrangle: Saylorsburg, PA

Sites 26–29

Sites 26–29 map showing roads and towns including Jim Thorpe, Lehighton, Palmerton, Danielsville, Kunkletown, Wind Gap, Saylorsburg, Brodheadsville, and Beltzville State Park. Routes shown include 33, 209, 115, 534, 903, 476, 248, 443, 695, 512, 567, 946, and Little Gap Road.

N

0   2 mi.
0   2 km.

Parking is on the south side of the road and is limited to one or two cars at the most.

Finding the site: Take PA 33 and exit at Saylorsburg. Proceed through Saylorsburg and continue northwest on Old Route 115, aka the Wilkes-Barre Turnpike, for approximately 1.1 miles until you reach the intersection with Anchorage Road. Pass the intersection with Anchorage Road to the north and Ross Road to the south, proceed approximately 800 feet, and look for the outcrops on the right (north) and a small parking area on the left (south) side of the road. You will likely have to proceed further northwest to find a safe place to turn around. Proceed back to the parking area on the south side of the road, park, and walk across the road to the outcrops.

Rockhounding

This outcrop is in the "Centerfield fossil zone" of the Middle Devonian-age Mahantango Formation. The fossils at this site include horn corals, brachiopods, and bryozoans. Look for the rocks that appear to have "worm holes" and voids, and split these open to reveal the fossils. There are also several barren zones in this outcrop and you have to make sure that you focus on the fossiliferous zones, but they are relatively easy to identify in the outcrops. Parking is adequate for one or two cars, but it is not a good place for large groups. Traffic is generally heavy on this road as well so you have to be very careful when crossing the road. As always, if the site becomes posted against trespassing, you must stay out of the posted areas.

References: Hoskins et al., 1983; Beerbower, 1957; El-Ashry, 1971

27. Beltzville State Park Devonian Fossils

Many of the fossils are fragments of coral.

See map page 94.
County: Carbon
Site type: Outcrops on shoreline of Beltzville Lake
Land status: State park, collecting allowed
Material: Devonian fossils, including brachiopods, crinoids, bryozoans, and corals
Host rock: Shales and sandstones of Devonian-age Mahantango Formation
Difficulty: Easy
Family-friendly: Yes, excellent to combine with swimming, fishing, and picnicking at the park
Tools needed: Hammer, chisel, flat-bladed screwdriver
Special concerns: Collecting next to a lake, but shoreline slopes are gentle
Special attractions: Beltzville State Park, Lehigh Gorge Scenic Railway
GPS parking: N40° 51' 30" / W75° 38' 00"
GPS shoreline outcrops: N40° 51' 24" / W75° 38' 03"

Fossils can be found in loose rocks along the lake shore.

Topographic quadrangle: Lehighton, PA

Finding the site: Take I-476 to the exit near Lehighton, which is exit 74. This is part of the Pennsylvania Turnpike so it is a toll road. An alternative is to take another route and get to US 209 east of Lehighton. Turn north onto Harrity Road, which is immediately west of the intersection with 209 and 476. The intersection of 209 and 476 can be very confusing, so be prepared in advance. Continue approximately 400 feet on Harrity Road, and turn right (east) onto Pohopoco Drive. Continue 3.0 miles east, and the entrance to Beltzville State Park is on right (south) side of the road. Enter the park and proceed 0.7 mile to Pavilion #2, which is on the north side of the western end of the lake. The fossils are in outcrops along the shoreline just west of the pavilion area.

Rockhounding

This is an excellent location to introduce young kids as well as adults to fossil collecting. The fossils are found in loose rocks and outcrops along the shoreline, and it is relatively easy to find brachiopods, crinoids, bryozoans, and corals. Fossils can be found on the weathered surfaces of rocks, but you may find additional fossils when you split open the rocks with a chisel or screwdriver. Fossil collecting is allowed in the park, but please be discrete and do not make large holes or lots of noise with your hammer along the shoreline. During my visits to the site, I stayed in the area of Pavilion #2, but there are likely other outcrops near the lake and along the shoreline that have the potential for fossils.

Reference: Epstein et al., 1974

28. Lehighton Lehigh Canal Devonian Fossils

This outcrop, located just east of the canal, contains several zones of fossils.

See map page 94.
County: Carbon
Site type: Former borrow pit and outcrops near old Lehigh Canal
Land status: Uncertain if public or private, not posted
Material: Devonian fossils, including brachiopods, crinoids, and bryozoans
Host rock: Shales and siltstones of Middle Devonian-age Mahantango Group
Difficulty: Moderately difficult
Family-friendly: Yes, scenic area, minor hike to collecting site
Tools needed: Hammer, chisel, flat-bladed screwdriver
Special concerns: Land status for collecting uncertain; ticks, briars, lots of barren rocks

The broad excavated area is just east of Lock #7 on the Lehigh Canal Trail.

Special attractions: Lehigh Canal, Lehigh Gorge Scenic Railway in Jim Thorpe
GPS parking: N40° 50' 25" / W75° 42' 09"
GPS broad excavated area: N40° 50' 32" / W75° 42' 17"
GPS outcrops and float with fossils: N40° 50' 33" / W75° 42' 20"
Topographic quadrangle: Lehighton, PA
Finding the site: Enter the southern end of the town of Lehighton via PA 443, PA 248, or US 209. These highways all converge at an intersection, from which you'll turn north onto Canal Street. Proceed north on Canal Street approximately 0.5 mile, and turn left (north) onto Long Run Road. Go another 0.4 mile north and you will see a small housing park on the left. Park here and walk approximately 300 feet to a small dirt road that descends to the canal. Approximately 700 feet down this road is a broad, excavated slope with shale. Proceed further down to the canal and look for float (loose rocks) with fossils and fossiliferous outcrops. The best float and outcrops are in the brushy areas near the canal and south of the road that crosses the canal. For reference, if you are walking up the canal, this site is just east of Lock #7.

Rockhounding

This site is listed in the 1983 edition of *Fossil Collecting in Pennsylvania* as part of the Centerfield Fossil Zone of the Mahantango Formation. The Centerfield is one of four thin fossiliferous zones within the Mahantango Formation in Carbon County. These fossiliferous zones are separated by thick sequences of claystone and shale that are largely barren of fossils.

During a visit in February 2012, I found that the broad, excavated slope was barren of fossils, as were many of the nearby outcrops. However, I found several pieces of fossil-bearing float in the small washes downgradient of the excavated area. The best pieces were saturated with water and dark brown, and I suspect they became saturated as the void spaces formed by the fossils made the rocks much more permeable. I investigated an outcrop in an area thick with briars next to the canal, and found fossils in this outcrop and many loose rocks with many excellent fossils, which were mainly brachiopods, crinoids, and bryozoans. I also found a tiny curled shell of a gastropod in the outcrop. The best pieces seemed to be under the leaves and are found as loose rocks rather than in outcrop. Look for the pieces that are dark brown and saturated, and split or crack them open to reveal the fossils. You may have to look hard for the fossil-bearing rocks, but they are worth the effort when you find them.

References: Epstein et al., 1974; Hoskins et al., 1983

29. Lehighton Quartz Crystals

Veins of white quartz with some clear quartz crystals can be found in the rocks at this site. The traffic in Lehighton can be seen in the background, indicating that this is a somewhat urban collecting site.

See map page 94.

County: Carbon

Site type: Former borrow pit

Land status: Private but not posted

Material: Quartz crystals

Host rock: Sandstone of the Devonian-age Mahantango Formation

Difficulty: Easy

Family-friendly: No, very sharp rocks, some highwalls, land status uncertain

Tools needed: Hammer, chisel

Special concerns: Land status for collecting uncertain, rocks are very sharp

Special attractions: Lehigh Canal, Lehigh Gorge Scenic Railway in Jim Thorpe

GPS parking: N40° 49' 20" / W75° 42' 49"

Topographic quadrangle: Lehighton, PA

Finding the site: Take PA 443 east into Lehighton. This turns into Blakeslee Boulevard Drive East. Go east past the intersection with Mahoning Mountain

The workings are open and easy to walk around, but you must be careful of some of the highwalls.

Road, proceed approximately 500 feet, and turn right just past a Pizza Hut on the south side of the road. The entrance to the borrow pit is just on the east side of the Pizza Hut. Park here and walk uphill to the workings. Most of the workings are south of the Pizza Hut.

Rockhounding

This site is a former borrow pit that was open and not posted against trespassing during a site visit in February 2012. The host rock is reported to be the Mahantango Formation, but the rocks at this site are very hard, dark, well-cemented sandstones and are quite unlike the softer shales and siltstones of other sections of the Mahantango Formation. Many white bands of milky quartz are within the sandstone of this site. In some areas the quartz veins have voids with clear quartz crystals. The crystals are generally small and less than 0.5 inch long, but many are well terminated. It takes time to find good specimens but the quartz is in abundance. A hammer and chisel are useful to have for cracking apart the rocks and field trimming.

Reference: Epstein et al., 1974

30. Deer Lake Devonian Fossils

This brachiopod was broken off a loose rock in the upper section of the borrow pit.

County: Schuylkill
Site type: Borrow pit
Land status: Private, posted on edges of borrow pit but not at access to main area
Material: Devonian fossils, including brachiopods, crinoids, pelecypods, and the trace fossil zoophycos
Host rock: Shales and siltstones of Middle Devonian-age Mahantango Formation
Difficulty: Easy to moderately difficult
Family-friendly: Yes, but this is private ground, may not be good for large groups
Tools needed: Hammer, chisel, flat-bladed screwdriver
Special concerns: Access may be closed at any time
Special attractions: Cabela's Sporting Goods Store at PA 61 and I-78
GPS parking: N40° 37' 17" / W76° 03' 34"
Topographic quadrangle: Auburn, PA

The borrow pit is just west of Highway 61 in Deer Lake.

Finding the site: Take I-78 to exit 29, PA 61. Turn left onto PA 61 north and proceed approximately 6.1 miles to the intersection with PA 895 west. Do not confuse this with the intersection of PA 895 east, which is farther to the south. From the intersection with PA 895 west, proceed north on PA 61 about 0.1 mile, and look to your left (west). The borrow pit is the first large open area to the left. Parking should be more than adequate at the pit.

Rockhounding

This is a former borrow pit that is a well-known locality for Middle Devonian fossils. The 1983 edition of *Fossil Collecting in Pennsylvania* also references a second pit to the north, but as of 2012 this northern site was an active shale pit and posted against trespassing. However, the southern pit, which is the one referenced here, was not posted at the access point to the main pit area but posted along the borders, indicating that the property just outside of the pit was posted. The fossils at the pit include brachiopods, pelecypods, crinoids, and the trace fossil zoophycos, which resemble rooster tails on the rocks. Many of the areas of shale in the pit do not contain fossils, so look for the obvious signs of fossiliferous zones, such as rocks with voids or shell casts on the rock exteriors. Break or split these open and you should find fossils.

References: Hoskins, 1969; Hoskins et al., 1983; Stepanski and Snow, 2000

Sites 30–37

31. Molino Devonian Banded Sediments

The banded sediments have reddish-brown to silvery-gray bands with crenulations that suggest some primary deformation when the rocks were deposited.

See map page 105.

County: Schuylkill

Site type: Roadcut

Land status: Uncertain, appears to be in highway right-of-way

Material: Banded sediments that have a crenulated pattern and silvery-gray color

Host rock: Shales and siltstones of Middle Devonian-age Hamilton Group

Difficulty: Easy

Family-friendly: No, limited parking and site is a roadcut, but good for a quick collecting stop if interested in collecting unusual banded sediments

Tools needed: Hammer, chisel, flat-bladed screwdriver

Special concerns: Traffic, limited parking, but collecting is done well off shoulder

Special attractions: Cabela's Sporting Goods Store at PA 61 and I-78

The roadcut is just a short distance away from the parking area.

GPS parking: N40° 36' 35" / W76° 01' 55"
Topographic quadrangle: Auburn, PA
Finding the site: Take I-78 to exit 29, PA 61. Turn left (north) onto PA 61 and proceed approximately 4.5 miles to the intersection with PA 895 East. At this intersection turn left (west) onto Rolling Mill Road and park on the shoulder. A small parking place is present on the south side of Rolling Mill Road near the site, but it will be necessary to make a U-turn to park correctly at this location. From here, walk to the roadcut, which is immediately north of the parking area. The best banded rocks are on the west-facing side of the roadcut.

Rockhounding

This is a relatively new roadcut that was constructed between 1999 and 2004, based on historical aerial photographs from Google Earth. The rocks at this roadcut are barren of fossils, but some parts of rocks have a unique banded pattern of thin beds that alternate between green, red, and silvery-gray sediments. The banding has some minor deformation that gives the thin beds a crenulated appearance when viewed along the axes of the folding. The crenulations may be the result of some primary deformation features during the deposition of the sediments. Some of the rocks are relatively hard and make excellent display pieces.

Reference: Wood and MacLachlan, 1978

32. St. Clair Pennsylvanian Fern Fossils

This fern fossil is typical of the ferns that can be found at this site.

See map page 105.
County: Schuylkill
Site type: Broad slope of former strip mine
Land status: Private
Material: Fern fossils
Host rock: Dark-gray to black shale of the Pennsylvanian-age *Llewellyn Formation*
Difficulty: Easy
Family-friendly: Yes, but this is private ground
Tools needed: Hammer, chisel, flat-bladed screwdriver
Special concerns: Requires advance planning, likely with organized groups
Special attractions: Yuengling Brewery Tour in nearby Pottsville
GPS parking: N40° 44' 25" / W76° 8' 51"

The former strip mine is relatively flat and gently slopes to the southeast.

GPS fossil area: N40° 44' 19" / W76° 08' 28"
Topographic quadrangle: Pottsville, PA
Finding the site: Take I-81 to exit 124A to PA 61 South, and proceed approximately 4.5 miles to St. Clair. When you reach St. Clair, turn left (east) onto Hancock Street. . Hancock Street soon turns into Burma Road. From the intersection of PA 61 and East Hancock Street, proceed approximately 2.8 miles to the parking area, which is on the right (south) side of the road. Park here and follow the trail, which heads southeast and then makes a sharp turn to the east. The trail then ends at the collecting area, which is a broad south-facing slope of a former strip mine.

Rockhounding

This is a classic, world-renowned locality for fern fossils. The fossils, which include other plants and stems as well as ferns, occur as white outlines on dark-gray to black shale. The white is the mineral pyrophyllite, which formed as pseudomorphs after pyrite. The best way to find the fossils is to look on the surface and split open large fissile pieces of shale. The interiors of the rocks that have not been exposed to weathering will often have excellent fossils. Many of the rocks have multiple layers of fossils, so you can often repeatedly split rocks with a flat screwdriver head and find more fossils. Once you find a nice piece, be sure to keep it in a controlled, weather-free environment as the pyrophyllite can weather away, leaving you with just a piece of black shale.

The St. Clair locality is listed in this book as it is a very important paleontological site, but you must be aware that this site is private, and it is very difficult for an individual collector to access legally. However, there are many mineral clubs and schools that periodically have field trips to the site, and your best strategy to visit this site is to go with an organized group that has secured permission from the site owners. An Internet search can often reveal what groups will be visiting the site during the year, and you can then plan your schedule accordingly. If you ever get the chance to visit this site on a field trip, I advise you to go, as it is uncertain if or when the site could be permanently shut down or redeveloped into a landfill or other type of site that would preclude access.

Reference: Geyer and Bolles, 1979

33. Suedberg Devonian Fossils

This fossil assemblage was pulled from the outcrop with a hammer and chisel.

See map page 105.
County: Schuylkill
Site type: Outcrops in former borrow pit
Land status: Swatara State Park
Material: Middle Devonian fossils
Host rock: Siltstones and shales of Middle Devonian-age Mahantango Formation
Difficulty: Easy
Family-friendly: Yes
Tools needed: Hammer, chisel, flat-bladed screwdriver, digger bar, shovel
Special concerns: This is a popular area, and you will likely encounter many other park visitors and may have to compete for collecting space. Old State Road is also unpaved and may be muddy. Two-wheel-drive vehicles should be sufficient, but be aware that parts of road may be closed at times due to flooding from nearby Swatara Creek.

The borrow pit is on the south side of the access road, and the best fossils are in the outcrops next to the creek on the west end of pit.

Special attractions: Surrounding areas of Swatara State Park
GPS parking: N40° 31' 19" / W76° 28' 45"
Topographic quadrangle: Pine Grove, PA
Finding the site: Take I-81 to the PA 443 exit, and take PA 443 approximately 2 miles west toward Suedberg. Turn left (south) on Swopes Valley Road, proceed approximately 0.5 mile, and you will cross the bridge over Swatara Creek. Immediately turn right (west) onto Old State Road, which is an unpaved road that parallels the creek. Proceed west on Old State Road for approximately 0.7 mile, and you will see a broad open parking area on your left. This is the former borrow pit. The best exposures of outcrops are on the west end of the pit next to an unnamed tributary to Swatara Creek.

Rockhounding

The Suedberg fossil site makes an excellent morning or afternoon trip when in the Harrisburg area. The site is a former borrow pit on the south side of Old State

Road in Swatara State Park, and fossil collecting is allowed at this site. The rocks are Middle Devonian-age sediments of the Mahantango Formation and were deposited approximately 375 million years ago. The fossils at this site consist of brachiopods, pelecypods, crinoids, and bryozoans, and trilobites can sometimes be found as well. Much of the borrow pit is weathered shale and you can spend time digging in many unproductive areas, so you should focus on areas that have exposed outcrops with fossiliferous rocks. The fossils are most abundant on the western side of the pit near an unnamed tributary to Swatara Creek. The site is a popular collecting locality and has many indications of previous rock hounds, such as pits and stockpiles of fossils. Loose fossils can be found on the ground, but the best collecting is done with a digger bar and extracting pieces of undisturbed material that may contain fossils. In some areas of very hard rock you may have to use a hammer and chisel to pry off the larger rocks. Look for areas that are darker brown and with small voids, which are often indicative of fossils. Split these rocks open with a chisel or screwdriver, and you may find they are loaded with fossils. The best fossils generally come from large rocks that are split manually, as the smaller rocks are often broken apart and do not have large intact fossils.

Reference: *Park Guide* 16, *Pennsylvania Trail of Geology* (no date available)

34. Sharp Mountain Boxcar Rocks

The quartz clasts of the conglomerate are prominent and make this a favorite place for many rock climbers.

See map page 105.
County: Lebanon
Site type: Outcrops on ridgeline
Land status: State Game Lands, no rock collecting allowed
Material: Quartz-pebble conglomerate
Host rock: Pennsylvanian Sharp Mountain Formation of the Pottsville Group
Difficulty: Easy hike, moderate climbing
Family-friendly: Yes
Tools needed: None, no collecting allowed
Special concerns: Rock walls can be very high, be very careful if climbing
Special attractions: Swatara State Park
GPS parking: N40° 32' 42" / W76° 32' 8"

The quartz-pebble conglomerate of the Boxcar Rocks form a prominent ridge along Sharp Mountain.

GPS boxcar rocks: N40° 32' 39" / W76° 31' 48"

Topographic quadrangle: Tower City, PA

Finding the site: Take I-81 to the PA 72 exit (exit 90). Proceed approximately 0.2 mile east on Fisher Avenue to PA 72, and turn left (north) Take PA 72 north for 3.5 miles to PA 443. Turn right (east) on PA 443 east, proceed 2.1 miles to Gold Mine Road, and turn left (north). Follow Gold Mine Road approximately 2 miles to the parking area and trailhead, which are on the right (east) side of the road. Park and follow the trail to the Boxcar Rocks. A GPS unit is highly recommended as the parking area for the trailhead is not marked.

Rockhounding

This site is not for rockhounding, as you are not allowed to collect rocks on Pennsylvania State Game Lands. However, this is a unique geologic site and is well worth visiting, even if you cannot collect rocks. The Sharp Mountain Formation forms a prominent wall of white quartz pebbles, and it is very popular with rock climbers. The rocks are an excellent example of conglomerate, and pictures of these rocks are very helpful to illustrate the concept of conglomerate and sedimentary rocks to geology students. The name "boxcar rocks" is very appropriate as when seen in satellite view, the rocks really resemble several railroad boxcars on the ridgeline.

Reference: Geyer and Bolles, 1979

35. Centralia Pennsylvanian Plant Fossils

Fossil leaves can be found by splitting the rocks apart.

See map page 105.
County: Columbia
Site type: Outcrops of former strip mine
Land status: Private but not posted
Material: Fossil plants
Host rock: Dark-gray shales of the Pennsylvanian Llewellyn Formation
Difficulty: Easy
Family-friendly: Yes, but steep slopes on hillside
Tools needed: Hammer, chisel, flat-bladed screwdriver
Special concerns: Slope can be slippery in winter, all-terrain vehicle (ATV) traffic, underground mine fire
Special attractions: Centralia, the town condemned due to underground mine fires

The fossils are found in dark shales on the north side of a former strip mine. The side of the strip mine is steep and you have to be careful on the side of the mountain, especially if conditions are icy.

GPS parking: N40° 48' 03" / W76° 20' 13"

GPS main outcrop: N40° 48' 02" / W76° 20' 04"

Topographic quadrangle: Ashland, PA

Finding the site: Take PA 61 to Centralia. On the south side of Centralia and west side of PA 61 is St. Ignatius Cemetery. Directly opposite this cemetery, on the east side of PA 61, is 2nd Street. Take 2nd Street, which is unpaved, just past Odd Fellows Cemetery, which is another local cemetery, and park. From here you can walk to the outcrop, which is approximately 800 feet southeast.

Rockhounding

Centralia is known around the world as the town that is on fire. In 1962 a fire at a garbage dump ignited a coal seam, and it rapidly got out of control. It is still burning more than fifty years later. The town has been condemned, and the buildings are all but entirely removed. What is left is a tourist attraction for those who like to see environmental disasters, but this is a somewhat small subset of the tourist trade: Do not count on finding any gift shops or restaurants in Centralia.

Plant fossils can be found just east of Centralia along the northern flank of a former strip mine with a very broad exposure of dark-gray shale of the Pennsylvanian Llewellyn Formation. In this area the Llewellyn has many fossils of the stems and branches of plants, and occasionally fossil leaves can be found. The rocks are relatively easy to break apart with a hammer, and a screwdriver can then be used as a wedge to break open the shale. You have to be careful with the screwdriver to avoid scratching the fossils. The exposure of the shale also faces south, which means that you will get plenty of sun and lots of good light for finding and photographing fossils.

Do be careful if you go to Centralia. While I did not see any indications of burning or subsidence in the area of the plant fossils or parking area, remember that this is an area with an active underground mine fire. For reference, my visit was in December 2011. Cars still use the main highway through the town, and the hills are full of ATV users, but you should still be on the lookout for subsidence, smoke, or other signs that you should park or stand elsewhere.

References: Arndt, 1971; Geyer and Bolles, 1979; Haley et al., 1953

36. Shamokin Whaleback Pennsylvanian Plant Fossils

Plant fossils can be found by splitting open the shaley rocks.

See map page 105.
County: Northumberland
Site type: Former coal strip mine
Land status: Private but not posted
Material: Plant fossils
Host rock: Dark shale and sandstones of the Pennsylvanian-age Llewellyn Formation
Difficulty: Easy
Family-friendly: Yes, but better for older children
Tools needed: Hammer, chisel, flat-bladed screwdriver
Special concerns: High cliffs on whaleback, known as local party spot
Special attractions: Pioneer Tunnel coal mine tour in Ashland

The whaleback and nearby syncline are among the most striking structural geologic features in the anthracite coal region.

GPS parking: N40° 45' 57" / W76° 35' 48"
GPS Whaleback: N40° 45' 50" / W76° 35' 43"
Topographic quadrangle: Shamokin, PA
Finding the site: Take PA 61 to Shamokin, and turn south on PA 125. Continue approximately 1.3 miles, and turn right onto Bear Valley Road. Continue west on Bear Valley Road. The road will soon become unpaved, climb slightly, and then come to a flat area. This is approximately 1.7 miles from the intersection of Bear Valley Road and PA 125. The trail to the whaleback is visible on the left side of the road. Park your car and hike to the site. It is recommended that you combine this with a GPS unit and aerial photograph to make certain you find the site, as you cannot see it from the road.

Rockhounding

This site is better described as a geologic feature than strictly a fossil plant site. It is an area where folded rocks can be seen in three dimensions. A whaleback is a descriptive term for a large mound or hill that has the general shape of a whale's back. It is also used to describe similarly shaped features in desert sands and round granitic mountains found in the tropics. In this case, the whaleback is formed along the axis of a large anticline, and is the dominant feature in this former strip mine. It is one of the most striking geologic features in the anthracite coal region. It is highly recommended that you stay off the whaleback as the sides are extremely steep and potentially slippery. Plant fossils, which consist mainly of stems and minor amounts of ferns, can be found in the loose rocks along the sides of the whaleback. The fossils are found in the dark-gray shales of the Llewellyn Formation. Nodules of hematite are also exposed in the Llewellyn Formation and loose nodules can be found on the ground. These nodules are extremely hard and very difficult to break open, even with a heavy sledgehammer. The site is also frequented by all-terrain vehicle (ATV) users, hikers, and local partiers, so in all likelihood you will not be alone when you visit this site.

References: Geyer and Bolles, 1979; Nickelsen, 1979

37. Dalmatia Devonian Fossils

Look for voids and openings in the rocks, which may indicate fossil-bearing zones, and split the rocks open to reveal the fossils.

See map page 105.
County: Northumberland
Site type: Roadcut/former borrow pit
Land status: Private but not posted, may be within highway right-of-way
Material: Devonian fossils
Host rock: Shales and siltstones of Upper Devonian-age Mahantango Formation
Difficulty: Easy, but site is well picked over
Family-friendly: Yes, but not for large groups
Tools needed: Hammer, chisel, flat-bladed screwdriver
Special concerns: Traffic on PA 147, but parking is very adequate
Special attractions: None
GPS parking: N40° 40' 44.0" / W76° 51' 42.6"
Topographic quadrangle: Pillow, PA

The fossils are found right next to the road, and parking is more than adequate.

Finding the site: Take PA 147 from Dalmatia and proceed northeast. The site is approximately 2.5 miles from the town on the right (south) side of the highway. If approaching from the opposite direction, it is approximately 1.9 miles south of the intersection of PA 225 with PA 147. Look for a broad parking area on the south side of the highway. The roadcut/former borrow pit with the fossiliferous shale outcrops is adjacent to the parking area.

Rockhounding

This is a small site that is notable in that it has adequate parking and the fossil-bearing rocks are right next to the parking area. The fossils are external and internal molds of mainly brachiopods and crinoid columns, and pelecypods and trilobites are also reported to occur at this location. The trace fossil zoophycos, which has a rooster-tail pattern, is also present at this site. The shale is quite soft and the fossils weather very quickly. While you can find some pieces on the surface, the best fossils will undoubtedly be on fresh surface of split rocks that are extracted from the bank. As this is undoubtedly private property, although it's not posted, please use discretion when collecting and do not make any large excavations.

References: Hoskins et al., 1983; Hoskins, 1976

38. Rockville Devonian Fossils

Brachiopods can be found in the Montebello Sandstone Member of the Mahantango Formation at this former quarry.

County: Dauphin
Site type: Former quarry on mountainside
Land status: Private, ownership uncertain
Material: Devonian fossils, mainly brachiopods
Host rock: Montebello member of the Middle Devonian-age Mahantango Formation
Difficulty: Moderate
Family-friendly: No, due to climbing and potential access issues
Tools needed: Hammer, chisel, flat-bladed screwdriver
Special concerns: Have to cross railroad tracks, heavy brush, ticks, poison ivy
Special attractions: Fort Hunter County Park in Harrisburg
GPS parking: N40° 20' 12" / W76° 54' 12"
GPS quarry: N40° 20' 21" / W76° 54' 13"

The quarry floor is overgrown with trees and the fossils are found in outcrops and as loose rocks on the ground.

Topographic quadrangle: Harrisburg West, PA

Finding the site: From Harrisburg, take US 322 north to the exit for PA 39, and go west 0.5 mile toward the Susquehanna River. At the end of this road, turn right (north) on River Road/North Front Street, proceed 0.9 mile to Roberts Valley Road, and turn right. Continue 0.1 mile to the railroad tracks and park just west of where Roberts Valley Road crosses the tracks. From here, follow the railroad tracks approximately 1,200 feet north, go under the bridge for US 322 and work your way up the hill approximately 500 feet to the former quarry.

Rockhounding

This is a long-abandoned quarry that was used for local highway construction, and it has been referenced in several publications. The bedding exposed in the quarry is nearly vertical and very resistant. The most common fossils are brachiopods, and many of the best fossils are found in loose rocks on the ground. Look for rocks that have void spaces that may indicate fossil-bearing zones, and split them open with a hammer or chisel. Many of the sandstone rocks are extremely hard and need to be broken apart with a chisel rather than simply split with a flat-bladed screwdriver. When I visited this site in late 2011, none of the ground that I crossed had any No Trespassing signs or other indications that access or crossing was prohibited, but this can change at any time. In the event the rail line or abandoned quarry become posted or fenced off, it may not be possible to enter this site.

References: Ellison, 1965; Hoskins, 1969; Hoskins et al., 1983; Inners, 1984; Sheppard and Hunter, 1960

Sites 38–40

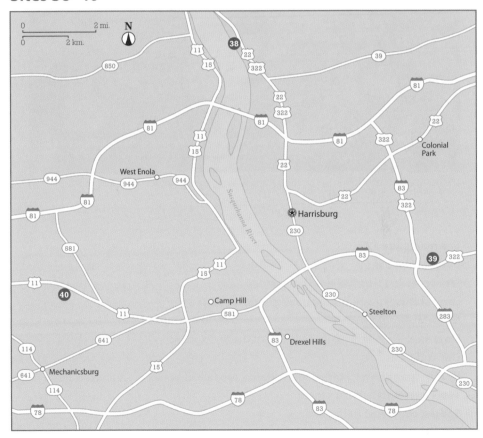

39. Harrisburg Boxwork Limestone

The boxwork limestone often has an angular shape as opposed to "boxes" with right angles.

See map page 127.
County: Dauphin
Site type: Roadcut and large boulders
Land status: Private, posted on west side of road
Material: Boxwork limestone
Host rock: Ordovician-age limestone of the St. Paul Group
Difficulty: Easy
Family-friendly: No, limited space, traffic, can fall off boulders and road walls
Tools needed: Hammer, chisel
Special concerns: Traffic, briars
Special attractions: Hershey Park
GPS parking: N40° 16' 06" / W76° 44' 53"
GPS outcrops: N40° 15' 59" / W76° 44' 51"

Small, loose pieces with boxwork limestone structures can be found on the top of the roadcut.

Topographic quadrangle: Hershey, PA

Finding the site: Take US 322 to the intersection with Grayson Road and turn north. This is an unusual intersection and Grayson Road actually goes nearly due west. Proceed approximately 0.1 mile, and turn north at the first intersection, which is with Milroy Road. Proceed north 0.3 mile on Milroy Road, and you will soon see a railroad overpass and a roadcut with gray limestone on both the east and west sides of the road. Go through the rail overpass, which is quite narrow, and park at the convenience store at the southeast corner of the intersection of Milroy Road and Derry Street. From here you can walk to the outcrops just north of the rail overpass, and just to the west there are also several large boulders with boxwork limestone structures near stormwater controls for nearby parking lots. Boxwork limestone can also be found south of the rail overpass, but parking is limited to private lots of nearby businesses.

Rockhounding

This site is a good opportunity to see boxwork structures in limestone. Boxwork structures are formed by fracturing the rock, and thin bands of calcite and quartz fill the fractures. The limestone is then later eroded, leaving the pattern of "boxes." Not all the limestone has these structures, and you may have to spend some time looking for the best pieces. Due to the traffic along this road, this site is best visited in very early mornings on weekends when traffic is at a minimum. Collecting along the road is extremely dangerous and should not be done, but it is possible to walk safely along the top of the roadcut. As always, stay away from areas that are posted against trespassing.

One cannot mention boxwork limestone without mentioning Wind Cave in South Dakota. Wind Cave is known for its prominent boxwork structures, and no other cave is known to have such well-formed and abundant boxwork. The boxwork structures seen at this Harrisburg site cannot approach the scale of the Wind Cave boxwork, but at least you can see them up close and in daylight.

Reference: MacLachlan, 1967

40. Mechanicsburg Cabbage Head Quartz

The rosettes can easily be spotted on the surface of the stream bed.

See map page 127.
County: Cumberland
Site type: Streambed
Land status: Next to park, unfenced, may be owned by US Navy
Material: Quartz rosettes
Host rock: No rocks in outcrop, but rosettes originated in limestones of the Ordovician Rockdale Run Formation
Difficulty: Easy
Family-friendly: Yes
Tools needed: None, but bring a hammer if you would like to open some of the rocks
Special concerns: Land status uncertain

The stream channel is generally dry and very rocky.

Special attractions: Stores along the Miracle Mile, which is the Carlisle Pike
GPS parking: N40° 14' 32" / W77° 00' 07"
GPS streambed: N40° 14' 29" / W77° 00' 06"
Topographic quadrangle: Mechanicsburg, PA
Finding the site: Take the Carlisle Pike, which is US 11, to Mechanicsburg, and turn south on Salem Church Road. Continue south for 0.5 mile, turn right (west) onto Salem Park Circle, follow this circle a little over 0.3 mile to a small park on the south side of Salem Park Circle, and park on the south side of the road. Do not park next to the mailbox on Salem Park Circle, as this needs to be kept open for mail delivery and residents. You can then walk to the site, which is only about 250 feet to the south. The pieces of cabbage head quartz are found throughout this streambed.

Rockhounding
This site consists of a stream channel, which is generally dry, that has pieces of quartz rosettes that have weathered from the underlying bedrock limestone of

the Ordovician-age Rockdale Run Formation. These quartz rosettes are not found in outcrop but simply lie on the surface with the other rocks in the streambed. They are white to light-tan crenulated rocks that are nearly entirely quartz with minor limonite and hematite. The rosettes have a banded, concentric structure that is sometimes arranged around a spherical quartz core. The rosettes have a colloform structure, which indicates that they may have formed from a colloidal silica gel at low temperature, which would be characteristic of near-surface conditions during formation. The rosettes are relatively abundant and are very easy to find. You do not even need a hammer, and the rosettes are usually relatively clean and not full of mud. Compared to many sites, this is very clean collecting, as long as you stay out of any wet areas in the stream channel.

References: Beard, 2006a; *Pennsylvania Geology,* 1969; Root, 1977

41. Boiling Springs– Reading Banks Cryptomelane and Goethite

Some of the cryptomelane has a bright metallic luster and an iridescent character.

County: Cumberland

Site type: Former open-pit manganese mine

Land status: Private, must get permission for access

Material: Nodular pieces of cryptomelane and "bombshells" of goethite

Host rock: Clay from weathered Cambrian Tomstown dolomite

Difficulty: Easy, but requires some hiking

Family-friendly: Yes, but must obtain permission

Tools needed: Hammer, chisel, small shovel

Special concerns: Ticks, poison ivy, hunters may be present during hunting season

The underground workings have long since collapsed but goethite and cryptomelane can still be found on the surface.

Special attractions: None
GPS parking: N40° 08' 12" / W77° 06' 40"
GPS north side of pit: N40° 08' 02" / W77° 06' 35"
Topographic quadrangle: Mechanicsburg, PA
Finding the site: Take PA 74 2.0 miles to Leidigh Drive, which is south of Yellow Breeches Creek, turn south onto Criswell Drive, and follow it 0.3 mile to where Criswell ends at the base of Long Mountain. Follow the trail in the woods to the south for approximately 1,500 feet to the former open-pit mine site. The property is posted but not fenced, and you should get permission prior to going on the property. I usually just ask the residents in the houses immediately north of the site, and I have not encountered any problems with getting permission to go to the mine site. Some appreciated that I asked for permission, as they reported that hunters often access the site without permission.

Rockhounding

This site is commonly referred to as the Reading Banks manganese locality and was mined in the late nineteenth century for iron. The mine ultimately closed due to the inability to process ores with high manganese. The mine briefly reopened near the beginning of World War II when manganese was in demand but closed again shortly afterward. All of the workings have long since caved, but pieces of cryptomelane and goethite can be found on the surface. The cryptomelane occurs as hard, black nodular pieces that sometimes have a botryoidal texture and an iridescent, metallic appearance. The goethite occurs as large brown to black pieces that sometimes form "bombshells," which resemble fragments of exploded cannonballs. Some of the goethite has a fibrous character on fresh surfaces, and the interiors of the bombshells sometimes have a boxwork structure.

References: Beard, 2006; Geyer et al, 1976

Sites 41–46

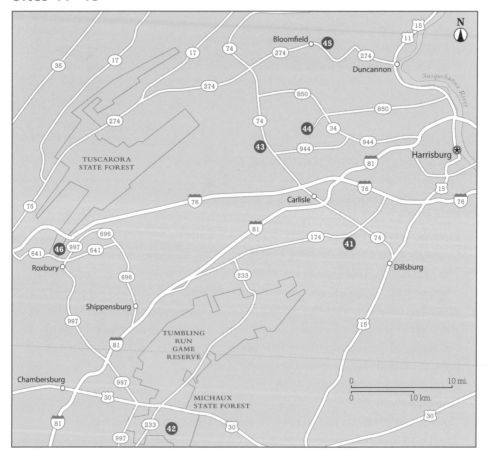

42. Carbaugh Reservoir Metavolcanics

The metarhyolite has a spotted appearance on freshly broken surfaces.

See map page 136.
County: Adams
Site type: Outcrops on hillside and rocks at dam
Land status: Michaux State Forest
Material: Precambrian-age Catoctin metarhyolite, columnar jointing structures
Host rock: Metarhyolite
Difficulty: Easy
Family-friendly: Yes, excellent scenery and interesting rocks
Tools needed: None, no collecting allowed
Special concerns: Dam site, highwalls at spillway. Road may also be difficult for 2-wheel-drive vehicles during wet or icy conditions.
Special attractions: Michaux State Forest, Gettysburg Outlet Malls

The columnar jointed metavolcanics are on the west side of the reservoir near the dam.

GPS parking: N39° 52' 22" / W77° 27' 02"
GPS columnar jointed outcrops: N39° 52' 19" / W77° 27' 07"
Topographic quadrangle: Iron Springs, PA
Finding the site: Take US 30 from either Chambersburg or Gettysburg, and proceed to Newman Road, which is approximately 300 feet west of the intersection of PA 233 and US 30. Take Newman Road south for approximately 2.3 miles to District Road, and turn west onto District Road. Take District Road 1.5 miles west to Carbaugh Reservoir, which will be on the south side of District Road. Park and walk to the dam spillway and dam. The columnar jointed metarhyolite outcrops are on the west side of the lake just south of the spillway.

Rockhounding

This site offers an interesting opportunity to see the Catoctin metarhyolite, which is a very hard, smooth metamorphosed volcanic rock that has a leopard-skin-like pattern. The rock is very hard and sharp, and boulders and large rocks can be found at the dam site and in the creek near the spillway. A short hike and climb

The rocks at the base of the dam have abundant metarhyolite.

is necessary to see the columnar jointed rocks as the tree cover obscures them, especially during the summer. Rock collecting is not allowed at this location since it is a state forest, but it is an interesting place to see these rocks as it has good public access and makes for an interesting family day trip.

References: Geyer et al., 1979; *Pennsylvania Geology*, 1969

43. Waggoners Gap Turquoise

The green turquoise mineralization occurs as surface coatings on the Tuscarora quartzite outcrops.

See map page 136.
County: Cumberland
Site type: Roadcut
Land status: Private, likely in highway right-of-way
Material: Turquoise coatings on sandstone
Host rock: Lower Silurian-age Tuscarora quartzite
Difficulty: Difficult, best for advanced collectors
Family-friendly: No, traffic on highway is dangerous, and rocks on slopes south of highway are also unstable
Tools needed: Hammer, chisel
Special concerns: Traffic and unstable rocky slopes, ticks in brush south of highway
Special attractions: Little Buffalo State Park, Audubon Pennsylvania Waggoners Gap Hawk Watch area

GPS parking: N40° 16' 36" / W77° 16' 39"
GPS outcrop with turquoise: N40° 16' 37" / W77° 16' 28"
Topographic quadrangle: Landisburg, PA
Finding the site: Take PA 74, aka Waggoners Gap Road, to the crest of Blue Mountain at Waggoners Gap, and park at the parking area near the tower on the south side of PA 74 on the ridge. If coming from Harrisburg, take PA 944 to get to 74 in order to bypass Carlisle traffic. The parking area is approximately 2.3 miles north from the intersection of PA 944 and PA 74. If coming from the west from the turnpike or I-81, it may be necessary to go through Carlisle to get to PA 74, but this only adds a few minutes to the trip. From the parking area at Waggoners Gap, you can walk to the outcrop with the turquoise, and additional pieces can be found in the rocky slope south of the outcrop. However, PA 74 is extremely busy, and you must be very careful of the traffic.

Rockhounding

This site has minor turquoise on the surface of the Tuscarora quartzite. The Tuscarora Formation is well exposed in outcrops along PA 74 along the ridge of Blue Mountain. The turquoise occurs as coatings on the surface of the quartzite, and the quartzite is extremely hard and difficult to break off. It is suggested that you leave these coatings in place for others to admire, and look for loose rocks with turquoise staining in the rocky slopes on the south side of PA 74. These loose pieces will also be much easier to trim and break apart. Be extremely careful on this slope as the rocks are very unstable.

References: Beard, 2007; Smith, 1978

44. Shermans Dale Devonian Fossils

This rock was packed with crinoids and bryozoan fragments.

See map page 136.
County: Perry
Site type: Roadcut
Land status: Private, but collecting areas may be partially in road right-of-way
Material: Devonian crinoid columns and bryozoan fragments
Host rock: Devonian-age sandstone, siltstone, and shale of Trimmers Rock and Brallier Formations
Difficulty: Difficult
Family-friendly: No, due to traffic along road
Tools needed: Hammer, chisel, flat-bladed screwdriver
Special concerns: Land status for collecting uncertain
Special attractions: Little Buffalo State Park
GPS parking: N40° 18' 17" / W77° 10' 59"
GPS roadcuts: N40° 18' 18" / W77° 10' 58"
Topographic quadrangle: Shermans Dale, PA

The parking area is just north of a one lane bridge that crosses a small stream.

Finding the site: Take PA 34 toward Shermans Dale. Just southeast of Shermans Dale, turn west onto Snyder Hill Road, continue 0.2 mile, and turn left on to Pisgah State Road. Continue on Pisgah State Road, which eventually turns into Losh Road, for 1.5 miles, and you will come to a small creek with a one-lane bridge. Park on the north side of the creek at a very small pull-off. The outcrops with fossils are on the north side of Losh Road approximately 200 feet northeast of the parking area.

Rockhounding

This site is private, posted ground along Losh Road, and you cannot enter the area of the outcrops without permission. However, rocks from the outcrops fall along the side of the road, and you can often find fossils in some of the rocks along the edge of the road, which is presumably within the road right-of-way. This area was described as an especially good location for collecting fossils, but I found that many of the rocks were quite barren. However, the pieces that contain fossils are very fossiliferous, and I found a rock on the roadside that was packed with large crinoid sections and bryozoan fragments. The best way to identify the fossiliferous rocks is to look for the dark-brown, water-saturated rocks that have indications of void spaces, which are often zones of fossils.

Reference: Dyson, 1967

45. New Bloomfield Devonian Fossils

Brachiopods are among the most common fossils at this site.

See map page 136.

County: Perry

Site type: Quarry adjacent to roadside

Land status: Private but not posted

Material: Devonian fossils

Host rock: Shales and siltstones of Upper Devonian-age Mahantango Formation

Difficulty: Easy when you find the right spot

Family-friendly: Yes, but bear in mind that access can change at any time

Tools needed: Hammer, chisel, flat-bladed screwdriver

Special concerns: None

Special attractions: Little Buffalo State Park

GPS parking: N40° 24' 54" / W77° 10' 30"

Topographic quadrangle: Newport, PA

Finding the site: From the intersection of PA 274 and PA 34 in New Bloomfield, take PA 274/34 South (they are labeled as the same highway on many maps)

The quarry is on the north side of Roth Road, and the best collecting is on the west side of the quarry.

for 0.7 mile to the intersection with Roth Road. Turn left (east) onto Roth Road, which is just south of where PA 274/34 takes a sharp turn to the south. The site is approximately 500 feet east of the intersection of Roth Road and PA 274/34. Parking is available on the south side of Roth Road, directly opposite the quarry, and the quarry is immediately north of the parking area.

Rockhounding

This is a small quarry in shales and siltstones of the Mahantango Formation. Much of the quarry is barren shale, but fossils can be found in the rocks on the western side of the quarry. The best way to find the fossils is to look for rocks that have void spaces or fossils on the weathered surfaces. A hammer can be used to break apart the rocks, and fossils can often be found on the broken surfaces. Most of the fossils that I have found at this site are brachiopods. As this is undoubtedly private property, although it's not posted, you should use discretion when collecting and do not make any large excavations, even though this is a quarry.

Reference: Stepanski and Snow, 2000

46. Roxbury Ordovician Fossils

Look for rocks with small voids and low density, which indicate the presence of fossils.

See map page 136.
County: Franklin
Site type: Former borrow pits along highway
Land status: Private but not posted, may be within highway right-of-way
Material: Ordovician fossils
Host rock: Shales and siltstones of Ordovician-age Martinsburg Formation
Difficulty: Easy, but many zones in the shale do not have fossils
Family-friendly: No, while parking is adequate, traffic is an issue
Tools needed: Hammer, chisel, flat-bladed screwdriver
Special concerns: Traffic on PA 641, land status
Special attractions: Michaux and Tuscarora State Forests
GPS parking: N40° 06' 59" / W77° 40' 30"
GPS fossils: N40° 7' 03" / W77° 40' 39"

Topographic quadrangle: Roxbury, PA

Finding the site: Take PA 641 and head west from Roxbury. This highway is also referred to as Forge Hill Road. Approximately 1 mile west of Roxbury, you will see a pull-off with some shaly outcrops—this is the parking area. The shales in this area are barren of fossils, and the fossil-bearing rocks are approximately 500 feet west on the north side of the highway opposite a house next to Blue Mountain Rink.

Rockhounding

This is an interesting site to find Ordovician fossils in the Martinsburg shale. The parking area, while it has extensive outcrops of shale, is largely devoid of fossils. The best place to see the fossils is in the rocks on the opposite side of the road from Blue Mountain Rink. There is also a small pull-off here, but it is opposite a house and it is probably best to respect the residents' privacy by not parking in this area. The fossil-bearing rocks are easily spotted as they have void spaces that indicate fossils are in the rock interiors. The most fossiliferous rocks are typically much lighter in density than the surrounding shale, and you can pick these up and open them easily with a hammer. A chisel or flat-headed screwdriver may be used to split open the rocks along bedding planes. The fossils at this area include brachiopods and crinoids, and fragments of bryozoans can also be found in some of the rocks. The hillside is quite steep, and you can easily find excellent fossil-bearing rocks on the slopes next to the road. I recommend that you stay well off the road and only look for rocks in the borrow-pit areas. The traffic along PA 641 is very heavy and it is extremely dangerous to collect on the side of the road between the borrow pits. Further west of the site, the geology changes dramatically from shales of the Martinsburg Formation to sandstones of the Tuscarora Formation, and these sandstones are devoid of fossils.

References: Hoskins et al., 1983; Stephens et al., 1982

47. Seven Stars Devonian Pelecypods

County: Juniata
Site type: Borrow pit with fossils
Land status: Private but not posted
Material: Pelecypods and brachiopods in shale
Host rock: Dark-gray to brown shales of Devonian Mahantango Formation
Difficulty: Easy
Family-friendly: Yes, but site is private and access could be a problem
Tools needed: Hammer, chisel, flat-bladed screwdriver

Sites 47–49

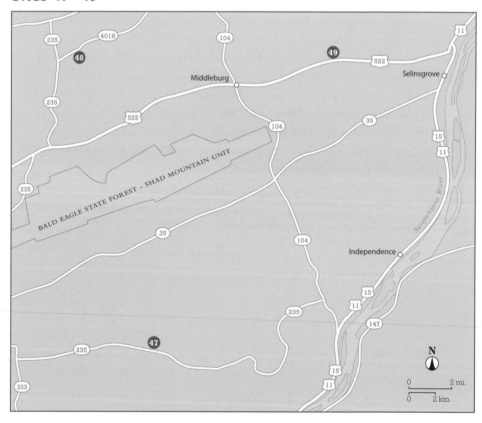

This site is well known for its abundance of pelecypods, which are bivalves with two "mirror image" shells.

Special concerns: Private land, may require advance permission for large groups
Special attractions: Little Buffalo State Park
Accommodations: Local hotels
GPS parking: N40° 36' 54" / W77° 07' 11"
Topographic quadrangle: Reward, PA
Finding the site: Take PA 235 to Seven Stars in Greenwood Township. The borrow pit is approximately 0.8 mile west of Seven Stars on the north side of PA 235.

Rockhounding

This is a large active borrow pit in the Mahantango Formation. During a site visit in January 2012, the site was not posted, but I did not experience any problems with collecting fossils near the road. This site is unique among other Mahantango fossil localities in that pelecypod fossils are abundant, especially the species *nuculites* and *orthonota*. The *orthonota* are similar in shape to the modern razor clam, and the nuculites also resemble an elongated clam. Small brachiopod fossils are also abundant in the rocks at the pit. The fossils occur as internal and external molds, as the original calcium carbonate shells have long been dissolved. Simply look for loose fossils on the surface, and you can also find them by splitting apart rocks that have visible planes of weakness that may be caused by the presence of internal fossil molds. If the site has been clearly posted against trespassing, do not enter the site without permission.

Reference: Hoskins et al., 1983

48. Walker Lake Ordovician-Devonian Brachiopods

This rock with iron-stained brachiopods was found along the access road.

See map page 148.

County: Snyder

Site type: Broad hillside with loose fossils, unpaved road with fossils

Land status: Pennsylvania Fish & Boat Commission, public access to ground, but collecting status uncertain

Material: Loose brachiopods that weather out of shale, and brachiopods in loose sandstones on unpaved road to spillway

Host rock: Calcareous shales of Devonian-age Lower Onondaga Formation and sandstones of the Ridgely member of the Ordovician-age Old Port Formation

Difficulty: Easy, but a 1-mile hike to site

Family-friendly: Yes, but children must be able to hike through brush and loose rocks, unless you focus on road collecting only

The access road has many brachiopods that can be found in the sandstone along the road.

The spillway area is just north of the dam.

Tools needed: Hammer, chisel, flat-bladed screwdriver
Special concerns: Hike to site is relatively long, hike to spillway requires hiking through briars, expect to get dirty in shale
Special attractions: Walker Lake
GPS parking: N40° 48' 18" / W77° 10' 48"
GPS spillway fossils: N40° 47' 57" / W77° 11' 52"
GPS collecting on road: N40° 48' 10" / W77° 11' 27"
Topographic quadrangle: Beavertown, PA
Finding the site: Take PA 235 to Troxelville and turn east on 235. This highway then turns into SR 4018. Continue east for 1.4 miles, and turn south on Westlake Road, which is a little over a mile east of Troxelville. Continue south for approximately 0.8 mile, turn right (west) onto Lake Road, and follow this 0.4 mile to the parking area. Park here, walk approximately 1 mile on the trail to the west end of the lake, and hike downslope to the fossil-bearing rocks north of the dam site. There is no clear trail to get to the fossils, so you can expect some bushwacking to get to this area. You can also find large brachiopods along the road to the hillside collecting site.

Rockhounding

This site offers collectors a place to find abundant loose brachiopods in weathered dark-gray shale and along the road to the hillside near the spillway. Collecting near the spillway is on the sloping hillside, and fossils are found loose on the surface and in small rocks that can be split apart with a hammer and screwdriver. These are Devonian fossils from the Lower Onondaga Formation. Do not dig in the spillway cut, as this is a dam site and holes should not be made in the soils near the dam. Many of the brachiopods found on the surface are small—1 inch in length or less—but their abundance makes up for their lack of size. In addition, the hillside slopes to the south, so lighting is good throughout most of the day and any snow in the area generally will melt faster on the hillside than the surrounding area.

The large brachiopods on the road to the site are also well worth checking out. These are Ordovician fossils from the Ridgely member of the Old Port Formation. Simply look for loose pieces on the road and roadside, and break them apart to expose the fossils. Some of the brachiopods are stained dark by iron minerals, but not all of the fossils along the road exhibit this type of dark staining. Do not approach the site from the west, as this is reportedly private property that should not be crossed.

Reference: Hoskins et al., 1983

49. Kreamer Wavellite

The wavellite crystals are small but occur as distinct spheres in the host rock.

See map page 148.

County: Snyder

Site type: Small former quarry on roadside

Land status: Private, well posted

Material: Small radiating "sunburst" crystals of wavellite

Host rock: Shriver member of the Ordovician-age Old Port Formation

Difficulty: Easy

Family-friendly: No, as this is a very small site and is posted against trespassing

Tools needed: Hammer, chisel, flat-bladed screwdriver

Special concerns: Private property, observing rocks limited to road right-of-way

Special attractions: Walker Lake

GPS parking: N40° 48' 31" / W76° 57' 35"

Topographic quadrangle: Freeburg, PA

Finding the site: From US 15, take US 522 west 5.9 miles toward Kreamer, and turn north (right) on SR 1009. This road is approximately 0.1 mile east of Middle Creek, so if you reach Middle Creek you have gone too far. Take SR 1009 approximately 1,200 feet north and you will see the site on the right (east). A shed that presumably contains telecommunications equipment is located at the center of the former quarry and can easily be seen in a satellite photo of the site.

Rockhounding

This former quarry is on private, posted ground, but the NO TRESPASSING signs are located along the hillside of the quarry. Under no circumstances should you cross past these signs without permission. However, the parking area along the roadside is quite wide, and some of this area may remain in the highway right-of-way. Small rock piles from the hillside are outside of the No TRESPASSING signs, and many of these contain wavellite. The wavellite crystals are found along the fractures of light-tan to dark-gray chert-rich limestone. Look for the pieces with fractures and voids, and crack these open. You may see small spherical crystals of wavellite, which is white to yellow at this site. Crystals that are broken reveal the radiating pattern of the wavellite. The crystals are generally quite small, ranging from $\frac{1}{16}$ inch to $\frac{3}{8}$ inch in diameter, but you can generally see the radiating pattern in hand specimens.

This site is listed in this book as it is described in the 1976 edition of *Mineral Collecting in Pennsylvania,* and it offers a unique opportunity to see wavellite crystals. However, you must respect the landowner and stay outside of the ground that is posted, unless you have received permission to access the posted area. I am uncertain of the land status of the parking area, as this may be leased by the telecommunications company from the highway department or part of the same land parcel of the former quarry. Due to the land-access issues, this should only be accessed by individuals or small groups with the understanding that access, even outside of the posted areas, is questionable.

Reference: Geyer et al., 1976

50. Danville Devonian Fossils

Brachiopods are the most common fossil at this site.

County: Montour
Site type: Roadcut with loose rocks
Land status: Private, not posted, may be in highway right-of-way
Material: Devonian fossils
Host rock: Siltstones of Upper Devonian Trimmers Rock Formation
Difficulty: Easy
Family-friendly: Yes
Tools needed: Hammer, chisel, flat-bladed screwdriver
Special concerns: Traffic, land access
Special attractions: None
GPS parking: N40° 56' 33" / W76° 34' 59"
Topographic quadrangle: Danville, PA
Finding the site: Start at the intersection of East Market Street and Railroad Street on the southeast side of Danville. Take East Market Street, which eventually becomes River Road, for approximately 2 miles, and you will come to a rail line

crossing the road. Park on the south side of River Road just west of the rail line. The hillside with the loose fossiliferous rocks is on the north side of River Road just east of the rail crossing.

Rockhounding

Fossils at this locality are abundant and you should have no trouble finding many excellent pieces. The fossiliferous rocks at this site come from medium-grained siltstone beds in the upper part of the Trimmers Rock Formation. These are known locally as the Stony Brook beds, and this fossil-bearing unit can also be found in Columbia and Northumberland Counties and at other places in Montour County.

The most common fossils at this site are brachiopods, and pelecypods and crinoids are also present. Look for loose rocks with fossil imprints on the side, and crack these open with a hammer or a hammer and bladed chisel or heavy, flat screwdriver. This locality has an abundance of fossils, but make sure that you do not spoil it for future collectors. If you collect at this site, make sure that you fill in your holes, do not cause any problems with traffic, and do not overcollect.

References: Hoskins et al., 1983; Inners, 1981

Sites 50–53

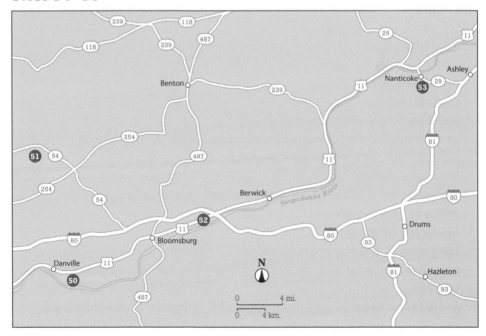

51. PPL Montour Preserve Fossils

This trilobite was found in loose rocks near the top of the broad hillside.

See map page 157.
County: Montour
Site type: Former hillside borrow pit
Land status: Part of PPL Montour Environmental Preserve, fossil collecting allowed
Material: Devonian Fossils
Host rock: Shales and siltstones of the Devonian-age Mahantango Formation
Difficulty: Easy to moderate
Family-friendly: Yes
Tools needed: Hammer, chisel, flat-bladed screwdriver, small shovel, digging bar
Special concerns: Large fossils hard to find, may have to spend significant time digging
Special attractions: PPL Montour Preserve Visitors Center and Lake Chillisquaque

The collecting area is a broad hillside and just east by southeast of the parking area.

GPS parking: N41° 6' 37" / W76° 38' 56"
GPS collecting: N41° 6' 38" / W76° 38' 51"
Topographic quadrangle: Washingtonville, PA
Finding the site: From the intersection of PA 54 and PA 254 in Washingtonville, take PA 54 north for 3.7 miles to Preserve Road, and turn right (east). Follow Preserve Road 2.7 miles to the intersection with Sportsmans Road. Take Sportsmans Road northeast for approximately 0.8 mile, and the parking area for the pit is on the right (southeast) side of the road. On the way to Sportmans Road, you will also pass Lake Chillisquaque, and right before you reach Lake Chillisquaque, you will see the Montour Preserve Visitors Center on the left, which is worth stopping at before you go to the site.

Rockhounding

This is a very large shale hillside where you can collect fossils. However, it can take some effort. Lucky collectors can find fossils on the surface, but your best odds are digging into fossiliferous zones into the bedrock beneath the shale fragments on the surface. You can crack open the rocks and may find fossils on the broken surfaces. Look for changes in the bedding pattern, especially any indications of voids, and break open rocks from these zones. If you do not find a good zone relatively soon in the bedrock after uncovering the rubble over the rocks, move to another site, as much of the rock is totally barren and you do not want to waste time in a section without fossils. I found a trilobite on the ground surface during my first trip to the site, so the fossils are there, you just have to look. The biggest advantage to this site is that it is a free site and collecting is legal, and it is an excellent site to bring kids (or adults) who just want to dig for fossils. I recommend bringing a hammer, digging bar, chisel, and screwdriver. If you visit the site during the summer months, bring lots of water and be ready to leave the area quickly in the event of thunderstorms, as there is no protection from the elements at this site. The hillside faces west and undoubtedly gets the brunt of fast, east-moving thunderstorms.

Reference: Stepanski and Snow, 2000

52. Lime Ridge Calcite and Early Devonian Fossils

The fossils are generally confined to the shaly area next to Low Street.

See map page 157.

County: Columbia

Site type: Former quarry adjacent to roadside

Land status: Private but not posted

Material: White calcite and Devonian fossils in shaly limestone

Host rock: Limestone and shale of the Early Devonian Helderberg Group

Difficulty: Easy

Family-friendly: Yes, but land status uncertain; collecting is next to roadside

Tools needed: Hammer, chisel

Special concerns: Site is surrounded by commercial businesses, traffic, land status

Special attractions: None

GPS parking: N41° 01' 49" / W77° 20' 59"

GPS calcite: N41° 01' 50" / W77° 20' 56"

Coarsely crystalline white calcite can be broken off many of the boulders on the north side of the small hill.

GPS fossils: N41° 01' 48" / W77° 20' 56"
Topographic quadrangle: Mifflinville, PA
Finding the site: Take I-80 to exit 241, and take the exit that leads to US 11 west. Proceed approximately 0.8 mile west and turn right (north) onto Low Street. The actual distance from I-80 to Low Street via US 11 may vary slightly depending on which side of I-80 you took the exit. As soon as you turn north onto Low Street, park near the small ridge next to the highway. You may also want to park near the rear of the convenience store on the west side of Low Street, which also makes a convenient place to get gas or cold drinks after your visit.

Rockhounding

This site has both calcite and fossils. The best calcite is coarse white calcite that occurs on the north side of the small hill on the east side of Low Street. It occurs in veins and along the sides of boulders, and generally must be broken out of the rock. The fossils, to the best of my knowledge, are only found on the west side of the small hill and are right next to Low Street. The fossils occur in a shaly section of the limestone and are best seen on weathered limestone surfaces. Splitting apart loose sections of rock in this area will generally produce some good fossils. Most of the fossils that you will find at this site are crinoids and brachiopods.

Reference: Hoskins, 1969

53. Nanticoke Concrete City

Coal fragments can be found on the road that lead to the Concrete City.

See map page 157.

County: Luzerne

Site type: Former coal company houses

Land status: Uncertain, may be owned by local municipality

Material: Coal, concrete

Host rock: No host rock, just concrete houses underlain by Pennsylvanian Llewellyn Formation

Difficulty: Easy

Family-friendly: Yes, but considerable offensive graffiti and potentially dangerous structures

Tools: None needed, rocks are loose on ground

Special concerns: Must be extremely careful in houses, as it is easy to hit your head, and some concrete floors, especially on second stories, have large holes and are falling apart

Special attractions: None, this is as good as it gets
GPS parking: N41° 11' 13" / W75° 58' 26"
GPS Concrete City center: N40° 35' 8" / W75° 20' 46"
Topographic quadrangle: Wilkes-Barre West, PA
Finding the site: Take I-81 to exit 164 and proceed west 2.1 miles on PA 29, which is also known as the South Cross Valley Expressway. Take exit 2, which leads to South Main Street, and proceed 1.1 miles west-southwest on South Main Street to Clarks Cross Road. Turn left (south) on Clarks Cross Road, proceed 0.4 mile, then right (west) on to Hanover Street, which is also SR 2010 and later turns into Front Street. Proceed approximately 0.7 mile on Hanover Street, and look for a broad pull-off that has space for a few cars and is directly opposite of a gated coal mine. Look for a trail on the north side of the road, and follow this trail north. The Concrete City is toward your left and slightly hidden by the woods. You can walk from the trail into the area of houses.

Rockhounding

This site has been included as a locality as many rock hounds enjoy visiting abandoned mining towns and camps. This is a large, long-abandoned coal company housing development. Pieces of coal and some hematitic sandstone can be found on the hike to the Concrete City, so the area also offers rock collecting, especially if you are looking for shiny anthracite coal.

The Concrete City was built by the Delaware, Lackawanna and Western Coal Company in 1911 using state-of-the-art concrete-construction techniques. It has twenty-two homes that surrounded a courtyard with a wading pool, tennis courts, playground, baseball field, and a small pavilion. While concrete is great for foundations and features that require significant compressive strength, it is poorly suited for walls and roofs of residential buildings. Concrete is very porous, and without proper sealing and insulation, moisture permeated the concrete and the buildings could become very cold. This resulted in peeling paint, mold, and a perpetual feeling of cold and dampness, especially during rainy and icy periods in the winter. The houses were occupied until about 1924. The Glen Alden Coal Company took over the buildings and did not want to upgrade the property with the sewer system required by the township. An attempt was made to take down a building with one hundred sticks of dynamite, but this had little effect. It became apparent that demolition would be expensive, so the buildings were completely abandoned and left to the elements, which included humans as well as nature. In June 1998 the Pennsylvania Historical and Museum Commission declared the

The concrete houses will eventually erode away, but at least they are now protected from demolition as they are a historic site.

Concrete City a historic site. This will help preserve this site for future generations to better understand the history of the coal industry and why you should not build houses out of concrete.

During a weekend visit in April 2012, the property was not posted. I observed several people, including ATV and bike riders, visiting the Concrete City. The houses, while they are still standing, are in bad shape and covered with graffiti, some of which may be offensive to visitors. I strongly recommend a hard hat to keep from bumping your head in the houses, and good boots and gloves are also recommended as the houses and surrounding areas are literally paved with broken glass and sharp pieces of metal. I also recommend visiting early in the day, as the Concrete City undoubtedly receives more than its share of strange visitors in late afternoons and at night.

Reference: Janosov, 1997

54. Bellefonte Ordovician Fossils

Partial stems of Ordovician crinoids can also be found in these limestones.

County: Centre
Site type: Roadcut and loose rocks
Land status: Private but not posted
Material: Ordovician fossils, principally crinoids
Host rock: Limestone of Late Ordovician Coburn Formation
Difficulty: Moderate
Family-friendly: No, due to traffic in area
Tools needed: Hammer, chisel
Special concerns: Traffic on roadcut, heavy brush and briars during summer months at roadcut, ticks and other insects
Special attractions: Fountain in nearby Bellefonte
GPS parking: N40° 55' 08" / W77° 47' 09"
GPS fossiliferous area: N40° 55' 13" / W77° 47' 08"

Topographic quadrangle: Bellefonte, PA

Finding the site: This site is on the northwest side of Bellefonte. For reference, the starting point is the intersection of PA 144/PA 150, aka Pleasantville Boulevard, and West Beaver Street. Proceed approximately 0.1 mile north, and the parking area is on the west side of the road. From the parking area walk approximately 0.1 mile north, and the fossiliferous outcrops are on the right (east) side of the road.

Rockhounding

This locality has some highly fossiliferous limestone. The best fossils are found in loose limestone rocks that have weathered fossils exposed on the surface. Hoskins

Site 54

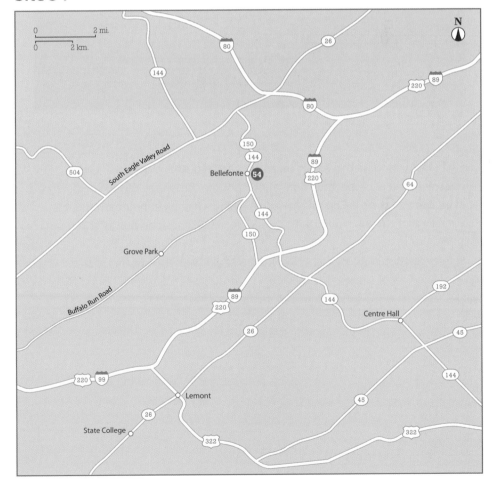

The rocks along the roadside are generally hidden in the brush.

et al. (1983) also says that fossils are present in the nearby outcrops of dark calcareous shales of the Antes Formation opposite the nearby sewage treatment plant and that there is Coburn limestone behind a nearby furniture store. But virtually all the fossils I found at this site were in the limestone along PA 144.

References: Butts and Moore, 1936; Hoskins et al., 1983; Thompson, 1963

55. Turnpike Devonian Graptolites

Graptolites can be found by splitting open the rocks and looking on the fresh surfaces.

County: Bedford
Site type: Outcrops adjacent to west-bound turnpike parking area
Land status: Shawnee State Park, uncertain of collecting status
Material: Graptolite fossils
Host rock: Devonian-age Brallier and Harrell Formations, Undivided
Difficulty: Easy
Family-friendly: Yes, but must be careful as you are adjacent to the turnpike. This is best suited for a brief stop if you are already traveling on the turnpike.
Tools needed: Hammer, chisel, small flat-bladed screwdriver
Special concerns: Adjacent to turnpike, potential for snakes in outcrops
Special attractions: Shawnee State Park, Gravity Hill
GPS parking: N40° 00' 45" / W78° 38' 49"
GPS outcrops with graptolites: N40° 00' 46" / W78° 38' 45"

Topographic quadrangle: Schellsburg, PA
Finding the site: The only practical way to reach this site is via the westbound lane of the Pennsylvania Turnpike. The nearest exit to enter the westbound lane is exit 146, which is at the intersection of I-99 and the turnpike. From this exit, proceed approximately 8.4 miles to the parking area on the north side of the turnpike. The site is a very broad parking area with several hundred feet of shale outcrops just east of the main pullover.

Rockhounding

When I first visited this location, I had hoped to find some typical Devonian fossils such as brachiopods, bryozoans, and corals, but I could not find any fossil-bearing zones. I had all but given up when I split open a rock and saw a curvy pattern, and I interpreted this to be a graptolite fossil. Graptolites were marine organisms that formed in colonies and typically had long branches with patterns that resembled

Site 55

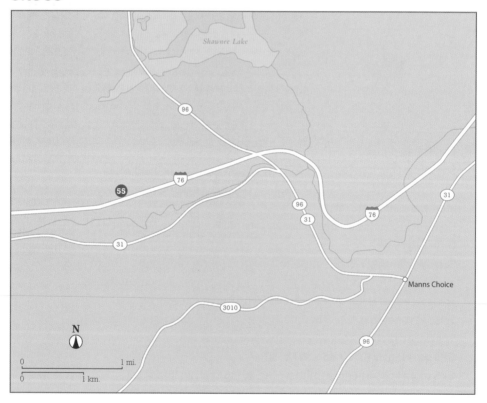

a hacksaw blade. The name *graptolite* comes from the Greek word for written, *graptos,* and the word for rock, *lithos,* as they somewhat resemble scratchy writing or hieroglyphics on rocks. They are commonly found in black shales and other formations that formed in deep water. You can find the graptolites by finding the large pieces of shale, splitting them apart, and looking for the fossils. A hammer, chisel, and a small flat-bladed screwdriver to split rocks are useful tools for this site. Some areas of the outcrop are better than others, and I have found the best sections were the ones with the most shale. Many of the zones are barren, especially the coarser zones, so stay away from the sandier sections in the outcrop.

You must also be extremely careful of snakes at this site. I did not see any snakes during my visit, but the site is a rocky outcrop that faces north, and small rattlesnakes love the heat and shade in these types of outcrops. It is very easy to turn over a piece of shale and be confronted by a cornered and very scared rattlesnake, so be sure to have sturdy gloves and keep your hands and feet away from potential snake hiding places.

This is a unique site in that while it is on the turnpike, it is located far enough away from the cars to provide for relatively safe access to the outcrops. That being the case, it is still important to recognize that collecting along the Pennsylvania Turnpike is illegal, as it is an interstate highway. If you visit this site, be extremely careful, stay well away from the turnpike, and try to stay outside of the field of view of drivers so you are not a distraction to them. In addition, while the site is adjacent to the turnpike, the ground with the shale outcrops may be managed by Shawnee State Park. While some Pennsylvania state parks allow fossil collecting, I have not found any information about the status of fossil collecting at this park.

Reference: Turley, 1952

56. Johnstown
Pennsylvanian Fossils

This is a piece of Brush Creek Limestone with a bivalve fossil and many innumerable tiny fossils in the matrix.

County: Cambria
Site type: Hillcut
Land status: Private, posted in northern part of site
Material: Pennsylvanian fossils
Host rock: Dark-gray Brush Creek limestone of the Pennsylvanian-age Conemaugh Group
Difficulty: Easy
Family-friendly: No, land status may be an issue, hillside is very steep
Tools needed: Hammer, chisel, flat-bladed screwdriver
Special concerns: Hillside is fairly steep, and while land is not posted, it is private land

The outcrops are well exposed in the hillside behind the shopping complex, and you can clearly see the Brush Creek coal and limestone beds.

Special attractions: Johnstown Flood Museum
GPS parking: N40° 16' 20" / W78° 51' 16"
GPS hillside: N40° 16' 22" / W78° 51' 16"
Topographic quadrangle: Geistown, PA
Finding the site: Take US 219 to the intersection with PA 56, and take the exit to go south on PA 56, aka Scalp Avenue. Proceed approximately 0.4 mile south, and take the first right into the University Park Shopping Center, and proceed around to the back of the complex. The site consists of the sloping hillside on the east side of the buildings for the shopping center. Note that the northern part of the hillside is clearly posted against trespassing and you must stay out of this area unless you have permission to collect in this section.

Rockhounding

This is a geologically interesting site as it gives one the opportunity to see a horizontal coal bed, overlying limestone, and another section of rocks with hematitic concretions. The coal is Brush Creek coal, which is a thin (0.9 feet) seam of coal. Fossils are found directly above the coal in the Brush Creek limestone. The limestone is dark gray and silty in the first foot above the coal, and then the limestone grades into a silty, shaly dark-gray limestone for the next 3 to 4 feet. Most of the fossils occur in the dark-gray silty limestone just above the coal seam. The silty, shaly limestone also grades into a dark-gray shale, and there are distinct layers of siderite nodules in this shale. The siderite nodules are generally solid and do not appear to contain many additional minerals, but they are interesting to see in outcrop.

Site 56

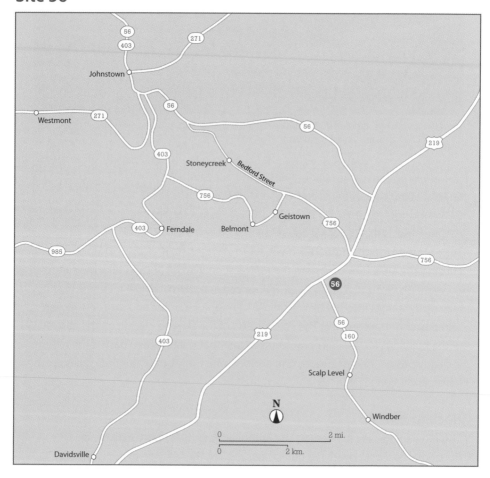

Since it is difficult to climb to the limestone, it is best to look for pieces of dark gray limestone that have fallen to the base of the hillside next to the parking lot. These can be split open and may reveal fossils. The fossils are generally very small, but occasionally you will encounter brachiopods that are larger than all the other fossils. Some of the rocks have also been pyritized, and these can easily be identified as they are much denser than the surrounding rocks and generally have a "rusty" appearance from the iron leaching from the rock.

As always, if you are looking at rocks near a strip mall or shopping center, do your best to visit some of the stores and give them some business. I generally at least try to get lunch if there are restaurants or tools if there is a hardware store. While the ground in this area was not posted as of March 2012, the parking area is part of the shopping center and is private property for the use of their employees and customers. If you visit this area, remember that the unposted areas of the site are still private property.

Reference: Hoskins et al., 1983

57. Uniontown
Mississippian Fossils

This large brachiopod was found loose on the ground in the underbrush.

County: Fayette

Site type: Former quarry

Land status: Adjacent to Pennsylvania Department of Transportation Storage Yard

Material: Mississippian fossils including brachiopods, bryozoans, crinoids, and echinoderms

Host rock: Wymps Gap Limestone member of Mississippian-age Mauch Chunk Formation

Difficulty: Easy

Family-friendly: No, requires some hiking around storage yard; lots of briars; steep slopes

Tools needed: Hammer, chisel

Special concerns: Land status uncertain, must stay away from highwalls

The former quarry is just northwest of the active PennDOT storage yard.

Special attractions: Ohiopyle State Park
GPS parking: N39° 50' 46" / W78° 38' 09"
GPS quarry: N39° 50' 51" / W78° 38' 11"
Topographic quadrangle: Brownfield, PA
Finding the site: This site is best described as near Uniontown, as this is the most easily identified nearby city when planning a trip to the site. Use a starting point of the intersection of East Main Street and East Fayette Street on the southeast side of Uniontown. From this intersection, proceed southeast on US 40 for approximately 4.1 miles, and look for a PennDOT storage yard on the left (north) side of 40. Make a U-turn and park on the north side of the road next to the storm drain. Parking is adequate and reasonably safe here. You are not permitted to access the site via the storage yard, but I found that the perimeter of the area is not posted with any NO TRESPASSING signs, and you can walk northward around the yard. The quarry is just northwest of the PennDOT yard.

Rockhounding

This site is an outstanding location to find very large brachiopods and limestones that are loaded with large fossils. It is known as the former J. V. Thompson Quarry, and the southern area of the former quarry is now a PennDOT storage yard. Many of the fossils have weathered loose from the limestone, and you can find large shells and other pieces directly on the ground, but the ground is also covered with very

Sites 57–61

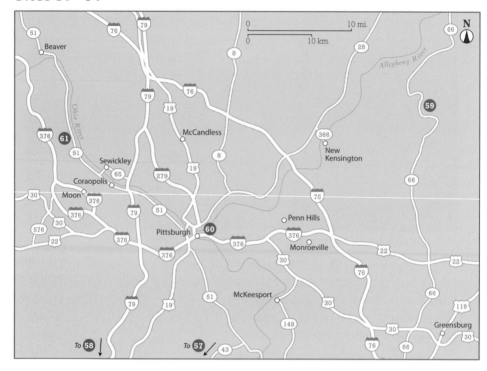

thick brush. Since the site is several hundred feet north of the highway, it is difficult to see the quarry, and I suspect that it is only visited by dedicated fossil collectors. I was able to access the area by walking around the PennDOT storage yard.

The best fossils are found on the slopes below the quarry highwalls, and you simply need to look for pieces of limestone with fossils in the underbrush. The briars are very thick in this area and I recommend good gloves and long pants, otherwise it will be a very painful experience. I also highly recommend visiting this site only after hours when PennDOT workers are not at the yard, even though the quarry is well away from the site buildings and equipment.

References: Hoskins et al., 1983; Hickok and Moyer, 1940; Simonsen, 1981

58. Carmichaels Pennsylvanian Plant Fossils

The plant fossils occur as black patterns and imprints on the shale.

See map page 178.

County: Greene

Site type: Shale in undercut stream bank

Land status: Laurel Point Falls Park, no posted restrictions against collecting

Material: Pennsylvanian plant fossils

Host rock: Pennsylvanian-age Cassville shale

Difficulty: Moderate

Family-friendly: Yes, scenic area, not much hiking to get to site

Tools needed: Hammer, chisel, flat-bladed screwdriver

Special concerns: Undercut bank may be unstable, nearby slopes are steep

Special attractions: None

GPS parking: N39° 54' 07" / W79° 58' 30"

Topographic quadrangle: Carmichaels, PA

Finding the site: Take PA 88 to Carmichaels, and turn east onto East Greene Street. Proceed approximately 400 feet, turn north on North Market Street, continue 0.2 mile to an intersection with a unnamed road on the right (east) that leads to Laurel Hill Cemetery. Drive to the north side of the cemetery and you will see a sign for Laurel Point Falls Park. Park near the sign. You can walk to Muddy Creek and the collecting site from here. The main collecting area is on the east side of the creek in shales in the undercut bank approximately 50 feet downstream of a small waterfall.

Rockhounding

This site offers the opportunity to collect fossil plants in the Cassville shale, which is a thin (12 feet thick) shale bed above the Waynesburg Coal. The best collecting is reported to be in an undercut stream bank just south of the waterfall. At the time I visited this site in early 2012, the stream bank was well undercut, and while it appeared to be stable, I was very careful when digging out additional pieces of shale to find plant fossils. The upper sections of the shale are very silty, and the coarse silty zones do not contain any fossils. I only found plant fossils in the shaly, fine-grained sections in the lower parts of the shale, and it took quite a bit of effort to find the plant fossils.

The fossils can be found by taking a piece of shaly material and splitting it along the bedding planes. A flat-bladed screwdriver is the best tool for this, but you have to be very careful to not put scratches on the fossils when you split the rocks. The plants occur as black patterns and imprints on the shale bedding planes and include fernlike fossils and horsetail rushes. I did not get to inspect the west side of Muddy Creek, but it appears that the west bank may also have the potential for plant fossils. The erosion in the bank appears to be due to both stream flooding and the myriad of fossil collectors that have visited this site over the decades.

The parking area is right next to Laurel Hill Cemetery, which can become quite eerie under the right conditions. When I visited the site in early 2012, the weather was quite stormy, and I had to return to the car early due to the lightning and rain. I was by myself and flanked to the south by a field of tombstones in a deserted cemetery. I felt like I was being watched, but I did not know who or what was watching. It became very dark, and I was reminded of the opening scenes of the 1968 film *Night of the Living Dead,* which I knew were filmed at a Pittsburgh-area

The collecting area is approximately 50 feet downstream of this waterfall in the shale in the under-cut stream bank.

cemetery. I thought that it was possible that this was the same cemetery, but it turns out the cemetery in the movie was at Evans City, which is north of Pittsburgh.

Despite the recent movies and news stories about zombies, the threat of a zombie apocalypse is practically nil at this site, as it is at all the other sites in this book. However, you may want to take the proximity of the Laurel Hill Cemetery into account if you have easily scared field-trip companions or excitable children.

References: Hoskins, 1969; Hoskins et al., 1983; Stose, 1932

59. North Vandergrift Barite–Sphalerite Nodules

The nodules often weather out of the shale in place and can easily be spotted and removed.

See map page 178.
County: Armstrong
Site type: Roadcuts
Land status: Private, may be in road right-of-way
Material: Nodules with barite and sphalerite, plant fossils
Host rock: Shales of the Pennsylvanian-age of the Casselman Formation
Difficulty: Moderate
Family-friendly: No, not much space next to road
Tools needed: Hammer, chisel, flat-bladed screwdriver
Special concerns: Traffic next to roadcuts
Special attractions: None
GPS parking: N40° 36' 18" / W79° 32' 58"

The nodules are found in outcrops along the north side of the road, and you must be very careful with the traffic.

Topographic quadrangle: Vandergrift, PA
Finding the site: Take PA 66 to North Vandergrift. From the intersection of PA 66 and PA 56, proceed south approximately 0.6 mile to Gravel Bar Road. Park at the parking lot at this intersection, and walk up Gravel Bar Road. The shale outcrops with the nodules are on the north side of Gravel Bar Road, starting approximately 200 feet from the parking area and continuing for approximately 400 more feet.

Rockhounding

The shales and siltstones exposed along the north side of Gravel Bar Road contain small nodules that sometimes contain barite and sphalerite. Many of the nodules are solid, but some have cores with white barite and brown sphalerite, along with limonite and minor hematite. Some of the nodules can be colorful on their interiors, but the majority of them are solid and dark brown. Plant fossils are also occasionally found in the shale. This site is best for advanced collectors that have the patience to find the best nodules, and it is most appropriate for individuals or very small groups due to the traffic on Gravel Bar Road. Barite, calcite, galena, and sphalerite reportedly can be found in the streambed next to Gravel Bar Road, but I was unable to find any significant mineralization in the streambed. The best pieces that I have found were from the nodules that are exposed in the shale along the north side of the road.

Reference: Lapham and Geyer, 1969

60. Frick Park
Pennsylvanian Fossils

The fossils in the Ames Limestone are tiny and abundant.

See map page 178.

County: Allegheny

Site type: Outcrops in streambed

Land status: Frick Park

Material: Pennsylvanian fossils

Host rock: Pennsylvanian-age Ames limestone

Difficulty: Easy

Family-friendly: Yes, safe place with easy hiking

Tools needed: None

Special concerns: Traffic in Pittsburgh

Special attractions: Downtown Pittsburgh

GPS parking: N40° 26' 14" / W79° 54' 28"

GPS outcrop: N40° 26' 04" / W79° 54' 14"

Topographic quadrangle: Pittsburgh East, PA

Finding the site: The site is in Frick Park, and while there are several ways to access the park, I recommend parking at the Frick Environmental Center as this is near the

The Ames Limestone outcrop is a horizontal bed that lies in the creek along the Falls Ravine Trail.

site and the trailheads. The parking lot is best reached using GPS, as the roads in the area can be very confusing. From I-376, take South Braddock Avenue north 0.9 mile to Forbes Avenue, turn left (west), proceed about 1 mile, and then turn south (left) onto Beechwood Boulevard, which then turns east. Continue 0.4 mile on Beechwood Boulevard, look for signs that take you to Frick Park, and park outside of the Frick Environmental Center. You then need to take the Falls Ravine Trail to the Ames limestone outcrops. The trails are marked and you want to be sure to take the right one, or you will end up walking all around the park like I did the first time I came here.

Rockhounding

This is a great site for anyone with kids who want to see fossils or an advanced collector who wants to see fossils in the Ames limestone. As a city park, this site is off-limits for collecting. However, it is still possible to see the fossils up close in outcrop, and there are also many loose pieces in the streambed. The fossils in the Ames limestone are generally very small but abundant, and consist of crinoids, small brachiopods, and small horn corals. The site consists of a distinct bed of limestone that lies horizontally across the stream, and it is approximately 3 feet thick. The Ames limestone is generally a greenish-gray limestone, and it is easily distinguished from the other non-fossiliferous rocks in the area, which are reddish-brown sandstones. Virtually every piece of greenish-gray limestone that you see in the streambed will have an abundance of tiny fossils, but you are not supposed to disturb any of the natural resources within the park.

61. South Heights Pennsylvanian Crinoid Fossils

The gully south of Highway 151 has Ames Limestone float and is safe from the highway traffic.

See map page 178.
County: Beaver
Site type: Roadcut and hillside collecting of loose rock
Land status: Private land but not posted, collecting near parking area
Material: Crinoid fragments in limestone
Host rock: Pennsylvanian-age Ames limestone
Difficulty: Easy to moderate
Family-friendly: No, lots of traffic, steep slopes
Tools needed: Hammer, chisel
Special concerns: Traffic on PA 151, briars, steep slopes
Special attractions: None
GPS for parking: N40° 34' 02" / W80° 14' 49"

Topographic quadrangle: Ambridge, PA

Finding the site: From I-376, take exit 48 to PA 51 east, aka Gringo Road, which is toward the Ohio River. Continue 1.4 miles to the intersection with Brodhead Road, and continue east on PA 51, now aka Laurel Road, for 0.7 mile downhill until you see a very broad parking area to the right. Park in this area, and park well off the road. The outcrops are on the north side of PA 51, and a broad gully with loose pieces of Ames limestone is just south of the parking area.

Rockhounding

The Pennsylvanian-age Ames limestone at this site contains abundant fragments of crinoids. The roadcut is extremely dangerous to access, and I recommend that you do not collect on the north side of the road. However, using the principle that rocks always roll downhill, pieces of Ames limestone should also be present as "float" in the gully south of the roadcut. Float refers to isolated, displaced fragments of rock on a hillside below an outcrop. The gully has a small, unnamed stream, and sure enough, rocks of Ames limestone can be found on this hillside. The Ames limestone pieces are generally a greenish-gray, clayey limestone, and they are loaded with fragments of crinoids. Many of the other rocks in the area are non-fossiliferous sandstones, and the Ames limestone rocks are generally easy to distinguish from the non-fossiliferous rocks. The area also has lots of slag that is the same color as much of the Ames limestone, especially in the western section of the gully, but the limestone is much easier to crack open with a hammer and you can easily spot the crinoid fragments.

At the time of my visit, the gully area was not posted against trespassing and offers an area that is relatively safe and outside of traffic, in contrast to the area of the Ames outcrops on the north side of PA 51. I would not recommend collecting at the roadcut on the north side of 51 at any time as it is far too dangerous. PA 51 is well traveled and almost always has much traffic, especially during late afternoon.

Reference: Hoskins, 1969

62. Franklin Siderite-Sphalerite Nodules

Many of the nodules, especially the larger ones, have large cavities full of barite and sphalerite crystals.

County: Venango

Site type: Roadcuts

Land status: Private, likely highway right-of-way

Material: Nodules with siderite and sphalerite

Host rock: Dark-gray shales and medium-gray sandstones of Mississippian-age Cuyahoga Group

Difficulty: Easy

Family-friendly: Yes, but must be careful of traffic; site is also very muddy

Tools needed: Hammer, chisel, flat-bladed screwdriver, bucket

Special concerns: Ticks, collecting site can be very muddy

Special attractions: Drake Well Memorial Park, Clear Creek State Park

GPS parking, south site: N41° 18' 10" / W79° 53' 20"

GPS parking, north site: N41° 20' 32" / W79° 52' 15"

The nodules are found in dark black, muddy shale and are easy to spot as they are generally a reddish brown.

Topographic quadrangles: Polk and Kennerdell, PA

Finding the site: This locality consists of a northern site and a southern site. Take I-80 to exit 29, then take PA 8 north to Franklin. In 2.3 miles this highway divides into two lanes. Site 1 (the southern site) is on the west side of the northbound lane and is approximately 5.8 miles north from where the highway divides. The southern site is one of the best exposures of shale on the west side of northbound PA 8. Site 2 (the northern site) is reached by taking PA 8 north and making a U-turn when the highway becomes a single lane again. Drive south, and the northern site is approximately 1 mile south from the U-turn. The northern site is a large, broad exposure of sloping shale on the west side of the highway.

Rockhounding

Venango County is better known as the birthplace of the oil industry than it is for mineral collecting. However, this site offers a unique opportunity to find large nodules that are often filled with siderite (iron carbonate, $FeCO_3$) and sphalerite (zinc sulfide, ZnS) crystals. The nodules weather out of the shale banks on the sides of PA 8. They can be picked up directly on the surface or pried out of the bank with a rock hammer or chisel. The nodules are usually light brown and contrast against the dark-gray shale, so they are easy to spot. A screwdriver or chisel blade can be used to split the nodules open to reveal the crystalline interiors. The nodules can range from a few inches to more than a foot in diameter and are generally irregular oval shapes and flattened. The shale is soft, and as it is dark gray, this can result in very dirty collecting, especially after rain or snow. It's important to keep your rocks in a bucket as the mud from specimens will get all over the inside of your car if you are not careful.

References: Beard, 2006; Geyer et al., 1976; Harper, 1999

Sites 62–63

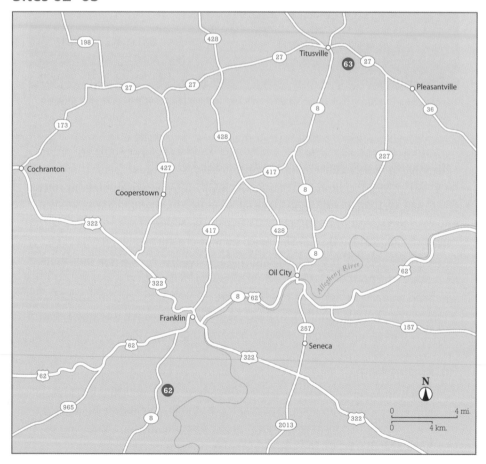

63. Titusville Mississippian Fossils

The outcrops next to the railroad are well exposed and relatively easy to access.

See map page 190.

County: Venango

Site type: Outcrops east of railroad

Land status: Formerly Oil Creek State Park, now part of Drake Well Museum, no posted restrictions against collecting

Material: Mississippian fossils, mainly very small brachiopods and pelecypods

Host rock: Mississippian-age Corry sandstone

Difficulty: Easy to moderately difficult

Family-friendly: Yes, but must be careful of railroad; uncertain of collecting status; good to combine with a trip to the Drake Well Museum

Tools needed: Hammer, chisel, flat-bladed screwdriver

Special concerns: Active tourist railroad

Special attractions: Drake Well Museum

GPS parking: N41° 36' 42" / W79° 39' 23"

Topographic quadrangle:
Titusville South, PA

Finding the site: Take PA 8 to
Titusville and turn east onto East
Bloss Street. Continue 1 mile on
East Bloss Street, which merges
with Allen Street, and follow
this across Oil Creek. Then turn
right (south) onto Museum
Lane, which in 0.2 mile leads
you to the parking area for the
Drake Well Museum. Park in the
parking lot just west of the rail
tracks. The sandstone outcrops
with fossils are in the woods on
the east side of the tracks.

Rockhounding

The rocks at this site consist of
outcrops of Mississippian Corry
sandstone that are exposed

This slab is covered with trace fossils and may have
some other fossils that I do not recognize.

on the east side of the railroad. This locality is reported to have the unusual
fossil *Titusvillia,* which is a branching sponge with cuplike nodes. However, the
only fossils I was able to find during a trip in late 2011 were small brachiopods,
pelecypods, and trace fossils. The sandstone splits into flat slabs, and the fossils
are most easily visible on weathered surfaces as opposed to freshly broken pieces.
Most of the fossiliferous rocks that I found were in the northern section of the cut
just north of the small train station for the tourist railroad. If time permits, a visit to
the Drake Well Museum is also recommended. The museum offers the opportunity
to learn about the early American oil industry and the Drake Well, which was the
first commercial oil well in the United States. The site used to be part of Oil Creek
State Park, but the land has been transferred to the Drake Well Museum. Although
I did not see any restrictions against fossil collecting, there may be restrictions in
place, so if you are uncomfortable with looking at the rocks, you should ask for
permission prior to exploring the outcrops.

References: Caster, 1934; Caster 1939; Hoskins et al., 1983

64. Union City Dam Devonian Horseshoe Crabs and Trace Fossils

Horseshoe crab fossils are the real prize at this site, but they are difficult to find.

County: Erie
Site type: Spillway cut below dam
Land status: US Army Corps of Engineers
Material: Horseshoe crab fossils, trace fossils
Host rock: Shales and siltstones of Upper Devonian Chadokoin and Venango Formations
Difficulty: Easy to find trace fossils and bivalves; very hard to find horseshoe crab fossils
Family-friendly: Yes, but must stay away from highwalls in spillway cut
Special concerns: Highwalls in spillway cut are sheer and you must stay away from them. Hard hats are strongly recommended at this site.

The spillway sides are very steep and you must stay away from the highwalls.

Special attractions: Presque Isle State Park
GPS parking: N41° 55' 14" / W79° 53' 51"
GPS spillway: N41° 55' 12" / W79° 54' 12"
Topographic quadrangle: Waterford, PA
Finding the site: From I-90, take US 19 south toward Waterford. Drive through Waterford, and at the intersection of US 19 and PA 97, turn left (southeast) to get on PA 97 toward Union City. From this intersection, proceed approximately 5 miles, and turn north on Middleton Road, which is a gravel road that leads to the Union City Dam. Continue north on Middleton Road for 0.8 mile, turn west (left) onto an unnamed road, and proceed on this road to the parking area. Walk west across the dam and to the spillway, which is on the west side of the dam.

Rockhounding

The spillway to the Union City Dam is cut through a thick section of nearly horizontal shales and sandstones. Bivalve fossils are common, and there are many examples of trace fossils in the cut. Trace fossils are the tracks and patterns made by the walking, resting, and dwelling of a wide variety of creatures, and they

Site 64

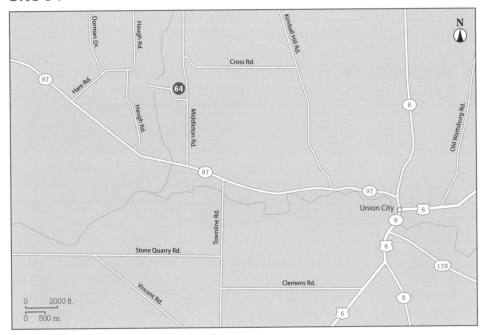

are very easy to find at this site. The real prize, however, is the horseshoe crab fossils. Horseshoe crabs, in contrast to bivalves, have only one shell with a hard side, so they are less likely to become fossils. The horseshoe crab fossils generally have a bulbous shape with ridges and a tail, and they have an overall shape that resembles a modern horseshoe crab. I have only found one horseshoe crab fossil at this site, but I am sure there are many more. Finding a horseshoe crab fossil at this site is largely a matter of luck, but you will find that your luck will increase the more time that you spend looking at the rocks.

References: Beard, 2006; Harper and Babcock, 1998

NEW JERSEY SITES

65. Mount Holly Iron Oxide Cemented Sandstone

The iron-oxide cemented sandstone is relatively coarse-grained and has colorful patterns, especially in the larger pieces.

County: Burlington
Site type: Small mountain with several trails
Land status: Park property but uncertain if city or county
Material: Loose pieces of iron-oxide cemented sandstone
Host rock: Middle Miocene-age Kirkwood Formation sand
Difficulty: Easy
Family-friendly: Yes, very easy hiking
Tools needed: None, collecting assumed prohibited
Special concerns: None
Special attractions: Burlington County Prison Museum
GPS parking: N40° 00' 10" / W74° 47' 28"

Sites 65–68

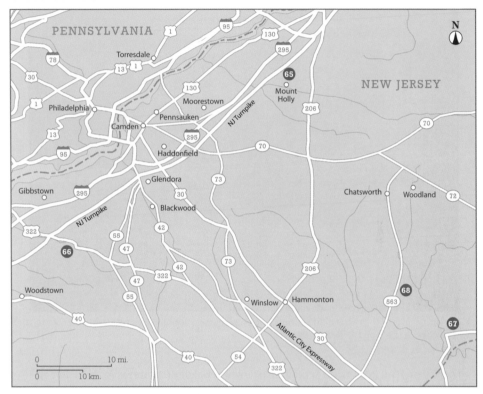

GPS top of mountain: N40° 00' 09" / W74° 47' 19"

Topographic quadrangle: Bristol, PA-NJ

Finding the site: From the New Jersey Turnpike, take exit 5 to CR 541, and head southeast toward Mount Holly. Continue straight for approximately 2.1 miles to Evergreen Street, and turn left (northeast). Evergreen Street leads to the north side of the "Mount," which is a prominent section of high ground on the north side of Mount Holly. Park in any of the pull-offs on the south side of Evergreen Street, and walk up any of the numerous trails to the top of the Mount.

Rockhounding

This site has loose pieces of iron-oxide cemented sandstone, which formed in the sands of the Middle Miocene-age Kirkwood Formation. The cemented sandstone is relatively coarse grained and well sorted. Heavy minerals, mainly sillimanite and staurolite, are also reported to be abundant in the Kirkwood

The trails that lead to the top of the "Mount" are short and well maintained, and large pieces of the sandstone can be found all over the summit.

Formation. The iron-oxide cement often makes lines and patterns in the sandstone, and the sandstone ranges in color from dark reddish brown to nearly brownish purple. The sandstone is all over the top of the mount and it is very easy to see. There are no signs indicating that rock collecting is prohibited, but as this is a park, it is assumed that no collecting is allowed.

Reference: Owens and Minard, 1964

66. Mullica Hill Vivianite

The dark blue vivianite is a strong contrast to the orange sandstone host rock.

See map page 199.

County: Gloucester

Site type: Stream banks

Land status: Private land, not posted, signs indicate it is a National Wildlife Federation Certified Wildlife Habitat

Material: Vivianite in nodules along stream bank

Host rock: Late Cretaceous-age glauconitic sediments of the Navesink Formation

Difficulty: Easy

Family-friendly: Yes, very easy hiking

Tools needed: Hammer, chisel, flat-bladed screwdriver

Special concerns: Lots of glass in creek, ticks, poison ivy

Special attractions: None

GPS parking: N39° 44' 04" / W75° 13' 38"

The nodules with vivianite occur in the steep banks of an unnamed tributary to Raccoon Creek.

GPS stream area: N39° 44' 01" / W75° 13' 45"
Topographic quadrangle: Pitman West, NJ
Finding the site: Take US 322 to NJ 45 and turn right (south) toward Mullica Hill. NJ 45 becomes North Main Street and is also known as the Bridgeton Pike. Cross Raccoon Creek and take the first right (west), which is Church Street. Church Street is approximately 0.6 mile south of the intersection of NJ 45 and US 322. Continue 0.1 mile on Church Street, and take the next right (north) onto Eric Street. Proceed north about 300 feet to the end of the street and park in the parking lot of the Raccoon Valley Swim Club. A trail along the south side of an unnamed tributary to Raccoon Creek begins on the west side of the north end of the parking lot. Follow this trail approximately 600 feet west-southwest, and look for steep areas in the unnamed tributary where the banks are exposed. The vivianite occurs in nodules along these banks.

Rockhounding

Vivianite is a hydrous iron phosphate (formula: $Fe_3(PO_4)_2 \cdot 8H_2O$). The blue of vivianite was often described as "Prussian blue," and artists have long experimented with vivianite as a pigment for blue paint. Vivianite has a hardness of only 1.5 to 2, so it was easily crushed and could be used to produce a beautiful blue. Unfortunately, as a hydrous iron phosphate, vivianite is also relatively unstable. It does not like light, and the blue crystals will darken to black and may even disintegrate. This is caused by the partial oxidation of ferrous to ferric iron on exposure to light. With further oxidation, the crystals will turn to brownish hydrous iron oxides. This actually made it a terrible pigment, as it would break down chemically and turn dark when used in paint.

At the Mullica Hill site, vivianite occurs as a secondary alteration product and has replaced the carbonate material in some fossils. The original fossils are difficult to see, but I have seen at least one belemnite fossil that was altered to vivianite. Many of the nodules occur in bright-orange sediments, and the dark-blue vivianite is an interesting contrast with the orange, sandy host rock. Since vivianite is so unstable, the best specimens are likely to be found in the walls of the banks, as the nodules that have fallen into the streambed have been broken and are often saturated with water. A hammer is useful to break open pieces to expose fresh vivianite crystals, and you may want to use a flat-bladed screwdriver for the more delicate pieces. However, if you collect samples directly from the bank, be careful to not make any large holes, which cause bank erosion.

Reference: Henderson, 1980

67. Bear Swamp Hill Quartz Pebbles

Most of the pebbles are solid white quartz, and it takes a little effort to find the translucent stones.

See map page 199.
County: Burlington
Site type: Small hill covered in white quartz pebbles
Land status: Penn State Forest
Material: Quartz pebbles, mostly white quartz, some clear quartz
Host rock: Middle Miocene-age Cohansey Formation
Difficulty: Easy
Family-friendly: Yes, easy hiking, quartz pebbles are everywhere
Tools needed: None, no collecting allowed
Special concerns: Long drive to site, must be careful of sandy roads and potholes
Special attractions: Batsto Village
GPS parking: N39° 45' 09" / W74° 27' 55"
GPS former tower: N39° 45' 08" / W74° 27' 56"

The area surrounding the summit with the fire tower remants is covered with white quartz pebbles.

Topographic quadrangle: Woodmansie, NJ

Finding the site: This is a fairly remote site and you must make sure you have a full tank of gas before traveling here. Assuming that you are coming from Batsto, take CR 542 approximately 4.4 miles to CR 563, and turn left (north). Continue on 563, aka Batona Trail, for 5.3 miles, and the road then becomes Greenbank-Chatsworth Road. Continue on this road for 1.3 miles, and turn right onto Lake Oswego Road, and take this 3.1 miles to Sooy Road, which is just past Oswego Lake and is a fork to the left. Continue on Sooy Road 1.8 miles to Bear Swamp Hill Tower Road and turn right (south). Proceed up this hill 0.2 mile to the parking area and summit of Bear Swamp Hill. The roads are passable with a two-wheel-drive vehicle during good weather.

Rockhounding

Bear Swamp Hill is literally covered with quartz pebbles. Some of these pebbles are well rounded and translucent and are similar to unpolished Cape May diamonds, which are found at the beach in Cape May, New Jersey. It is relatively easy to spot the translucent stones, which may take a good polish, but the vast majority of the pebbles are rough white quartz. Some minor subangular feldspar pebbles are also present at the site. The summit of the area has the footings of a former fire tower, and the small paths that lead up to this area are also covered in quartz pebbles. The easiest way to spot the pebbles that are similar to Cape May diamonds is to look on the surface for the translucent stones. However, you must also remember that this is part of Penn State Forest, and as such, collecting and disturbance of the surface is prohibited at this site.

When I first saw the remnants of the fire tower, I thought it was simply another tower that had been taken down for scrap. At the time I was unaware of a very sad but important part of the history of Bear Swamp Hill. On January 16, 1971, an F-105 Thunderchief from McGuire AFB was on a practice bombing run at nearby Warren Grove. In late morning the plane struck some trees about 100 feet south of the fire tower and then hit the tower and a generator building at base of the tower. The plane careened through the tower and the woods for another 0.8 mile, ending near the Papoose Branch. The pilot was Major William F. Dimas, age 36, who left a wife, two sons, and a daughter when he was killed in the crash.

The US Air Force sent the New Jersey Bureau of Forestry a claim form so that the NJBF could file a claim for reimbursement of the tower, generator building, and the nearly 1,000 trees that were destroyed. The claim, which was for nearly $20,000, was then denied by the USAF. Major Dimas was flying for the New Jersey Air National Guard, which technically made him an employee of the state of New Jersey. Property damage caused by members of an ANG unit who were employees of the claimant state was excluded from payment. After having this claim denied, it is not surprising that the state never rebuilt the tower.

Small fragments of the aircraft can reportedly still be seen along the path of the crash site. The plane's landing gear, which is slowly sinking into the mud, is also reported to be present in the woods, and there are many references to the crash location in online forums about airplane wreckage sites. I have not had the opportunity to visit any of the wreckage, but if you visit, remember that it represents a military crash site and must be respected as such. When I learned about this accident, it struck home as in 1971 I was living in Mount Holly, New Jersey, and my father, who has since passed away, was stationed at McGuire AFB as a major in the USAF. He was almost the exact age as Major Dimas. I never knew if he knew Major Dimas or if he remembered the accident, and I will never know.

Reference: DeCoste and Dupont, 2009

68. Harrisville Pond Bog Iron

Bog iron ore can be found around the sides of the old foundation near the parking area.

See map page 199.

County: Burlington

Site type: Loose rocks exposed in excavation for former building

Land status: Wharton State Forest

Material: Loose "bog iron" on ground surface

Host rock: Tertiary-age Cohansey sandstone

Difficulty: Easy

Family-friendly: Yes, very easy hiking

Tools needed: None, collecting not allowed

Special concerns: Can get stuck in sandy roads if you go exploring

Special attractions: Batsto Village

GPS parking: N39° 39' 40" / W74° 31' 19"

GPS bog iron at old foundation: N39° 39' 38" / W74° 31' 21"

The mansion is a prominent structure in Batsto village, which is worth visiting when in the bog iron region.

Topographic quadrangle: Jenkins, NJ
Finding the site: Many trips to Wharton State Forest start with a trip to Batsto Village, so the directions start at Batsto. From Batsto, take CR 542 4.4 miles to the intersection with CR 563, and turn left (northeast). Continue on 563, aka the Batona Trail, for 5.2 miles to the intersection with CR 679, and turn right (south). CR 679 is also known as Chatsworth Road. Drive 1.7 miles on CR 679 and turn right (west) onto Bodine Field Road. Drive to the markers that indicate an AT&T cable crossing, and park in this area. The bog iron can be found near a small foundation between this sand road, the AT&T markers, and Chatsworth Road.

Rockhounding

This particular site was described in the latest edition of *Gem Trails of Pennsylvania and New Jersey*, by Stepanski and Snow (2000). The bog iron ore consists of poorly sorted, well-cemented sandstone with abundant limonite and hematite. The pieces are found loose on the ground in and around the excavation for the foundation of a very old structure. They are not terribly interesting from a

The iron ore is generally poorly sorted sandstone and a distinct dark brown.

mineralogical point of view, but they provide a window into the early days of iron mining in the United States. Bog iron can undoubtedly be found in the many other areas of the forest.

Batsto Village is a former iron-making and glassmaking town that is now a nationally recognized historic site. Iron production began around 1766, and the Batsto works produced supplies for the Continental Army. Iron production ceased in the mid-1800s, and the town soon focused on glassmaking, which soon also ceased. The State of New Jersey bought the town in the 1950s, and the last resident did not finally leave until 1989. A trip to Batsto is well worth the time to get a better understanding of the area history with respect to the mining of bog iron.

Reference: Stepanski and Snow, 2000

69. Cape May Diamonds

County: Cape May
Site type: Beach with clear quartz pebbles
Land status: Sunset Beach, public access
Material: Clear quartz pebbles
Host rock: Beach sand
Difficulty: Easy
Family-friendly: Yes, very easy hiking
Tools needed: Small bucket or ziplock plastic sandwich bags
Special concerns: Beach tags required, no lifeguards, beach not good for swimming
Special attractions: Cape May region, many other beaches and activities
GPS parking: N38° 56' 40" / W74° 58' 12"
Topographic quadrangle: Cape May, NJ
Finding the site: Take the Garden State Parkway or other New Jersey highways to the extreme southeastern tip of New Jersey at Cape May. In Cape May take CR 606 west, and follow this 2.6 miles to Sunset Beach, and park at the Sunset Beach Gift Shop. Sunset Beach, which has the Cape May Diamonds, is just south of the gift shop.

Rockhounding

Cape May diamonds are water-clear rounded pebbles of quartz. They originated in the upper reaches of the Delaware River Basin and the crystalline rocks of New Jersey and New York and made the extremely long journey to the tip of Cape May and Sunset Beach. When tumbled and polished correctly, they strongly resemble a diamond, at least at first glance. I highly recommend stopping in the Sunset Beach Gift Shop to see some finished Cape May diamonds as well as some unpolished stones before collecting, so you'll have a better understanding of what to look for on Sunset Beach. I also recommend bringing some small plastic sandwich bags to collect your quartz pebbles, as your pockets are likely to fill up very quickly.

Another interesting attraction at Sunset Beach is the *Atlantus* shipwreck. Due to the critical shortage of steel in World War I, the federal government built an emergency fleet of concrete ships. In the early twentieth century, concrete was being used extensively in construction (see "Nanticoke Concrete City", Site 53 in this book) and in manufacturing, and many things were built of concrete that probably should have used other materials or not have been constructed at all. The concrete ship *Atlantus* was one of the later ships of the Concrete Fleet and was launched in 1918. In 1926, while it was being positioned for use as a ferry dock, the ship was caught in very bad weather and ran aground just off Sunset Beach. The remnants of the wreck can be seen for now, but it will not be long before it is washed out of view.

References: Beard, 2002; Stepanski and Snow, 2000

Site 69

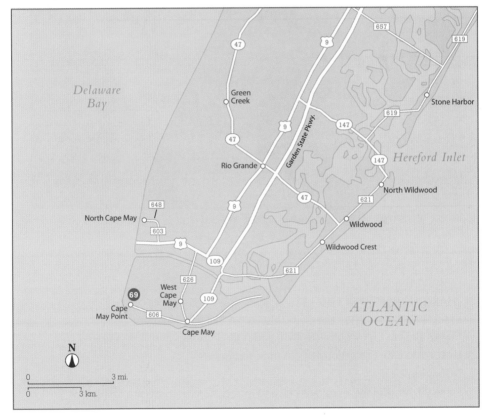

70. Big Brook Late Cretaceous Fossils

Belemnite fossils are generally easy to find in Big Brook.

County: Monmouth

Site type: Streambed

Land status: Park property, collecting allowed with restrictions

Material: Late Cretaceous fossils, including belemnites and sharks' teeth

Host rock: Late Cretaceous-age marine sediments

Difficulty: Easy

Family-friendly: Yes, excellent place to introduce newcomers to fossils

Tools needed: Screen, hand trowel

Special concerns: Will get wet, heavy brush, briars, ticks

Special attractions: None

GPS parking: N40° 19' 12" / W74° 12' 50"

Topographic quadrangle: Marlboro, NJ

Big Brook is quite high in this photograph. Collecting is much easier when the water is low.

Finding the site: Take NJ 18 to exit 25 and proceed north 0.4 miles on SR 79, aka South Main Street. Turn right (east) on Vanderburg Road, and continue 1.9 miles to the intersection with Hillsdale Road. Turn left (north), proceed approximately 0.6 mile, cross Big Brook, and parking areas to access the site are on both sides of the road just north of Big Brook.

Rockhounding

This is an excellent collecting site for late Cretaceous fossils in a streambed. The fossils include belemnites and sharks' teeth and are found by taking gravel and sediment from the stream and sifting it with a screen. Fossil collecting is allowed at this site, albeit with some restrictions. The site is managed by the Department of Recreation and Parks of Colts Neck Township, and the restrictions are clearly posted by the parking area. In brief, trowels are limited to a maximum blade size of 6 inches, and screens must not have a surface area of greater than 18 square inches. I think this might be a misprint, as I have seen other guides that indicate that the screens are limited to 18 inches on one side, which is

Sites 70–71

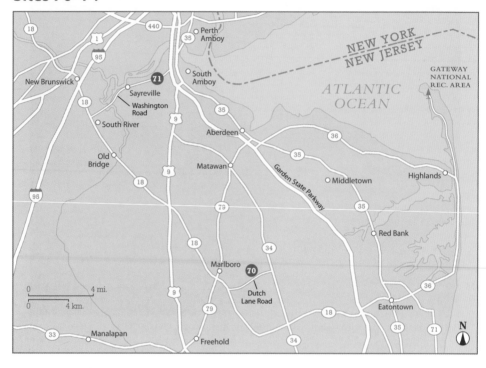

more reasonable. An 18-square-inch screen would only have sides that are approximately 4.3 inches long, and this would be about the size of a hand and quite difficult to use for looking for fossils. Groups of fifteen or more also require a permit from the township, which requires a fee. The collecting must only be done in unconsolidated material of the streambed, and digging into the banks is not allowed due to potential for further erosion of the stream banks. The best collecting is undoubtedly during periods of low stream flow when gravels are most easily accessed.

Reference: Stepanski and Snow, 2000

71. Sayreville Marcasite and Amber

Marcasite is also referred to as "white pyrite," and some of the specimens have a bright metallic luster when the clay is washed away.

See map page 214.
County: Middlesex
Site type: Holes in clay pits
Land status: Private land, not posted
Material: Marcasite and amber
Host rock: Late Cretaceous-age Raritan Formation
Difficulty: Marcasite very easy, amber more difficult
Family-friendly: Yes, but pits can be very muddy
Tools needed: Shovel, buckets, gloves, change of clothes, ziplock bags
Special concerns: Private land, status uncertain, will get incredibly muddy digging pits
Special attractions: None

GPS parking: N40° 28' 02" / W74° 19' 28"
GPS clay pits: N40° 28' 07" / W74° 19' 35"
Topographic quadrangle: South Amboy, NJ-NY
Finding the site: The area is surrounded by major highways and the key is to take one of the many area exits that will get you to Washington Road. A good starting point is from NJ 18. From NJ 18 southwest of Sayreville, take Washington Road approximately 4 miles to Lakeview Drive, and turn north. Proceed 0.4 mile to the end of Lakeview Drive and park along the street. Take a short walk north along the path that parallels the railroad tracks, and take the first large path that crosses the tracks. Walk northwest toward the barren area and you will see several pits. This is the main location for the marcasite and amber.

Rockhounding

This site offers two very different types of collecting opportunities. The location is very easy to find, as the clay pits are quite distinct. The two main types of material that you will find at this site are marcasite and amber, which are found near the surface of the Sayreville Clay member of the Raritan Formation.

As you approach the site, you will see silvery white spots on the ground. These are marcasite nodules that are found near the surface. Marcasite is an iron sulfide (FeS_2) that forms in the orthorhombic crystal system, as opposed to pyrite, which forms in the cubic crystal system. Marcasite forms under acidic, low-temperature conditions and is relatively unstable. If you collect marcasite, be sure to keep it dry and out of humid environments, as it will degrade and crumble to powder fairly quickly. The marcasite nodules are easy to spot and can be picked up off the ground surface. They are often covered with a white powder, which is likely melanterite, a secondary iron sulfate mineral. I recommend a large ziplock bag as the nodules invariably have at least one side that is covered with gray, sticky clay. You can easily find several large pieces of marcasite within a few minutes at the site, and you can collect it without getting very dirty, as long as you put it in a bag or bucket.

Amber offers the other collecting opportunity, and this is much more difficult. The amber occurs in lignite fragments and in some of the marcasite nodules in the clay. You will have to dig if you are going to collect amber, unless you get very lucky and find a piece on the surface. The pits have dark-gray sticky clay, and groundwater is just below the surface. The groundwater in many of the pits is stained brown to black from the lignite, and just touching the clay will quickly get it all over your hands and clothes. During my visit to the site, I

When you see the clay pits, you know you are at the right spot.

looked for amber on the surface but did not find any. I took several large pieces of clay with dark wood and lignite fragments along with muddy pieces of marcasite back home to screen and wash, and the only amber that I found was a 2-millimeter-size fragment that was embedded in one of my pieces of marcasite. However, other collectors have found amber at this site, and the amber is reported to frequently contain gnat-like insects.

In addition to a change of clothes, I recommend bringing a large plastic bag to put your clay-stained clothes in, and I would also seriously consider scrapping your clothes if they get too filled with clay. I found the clay very difficult to even wash off my hands, and it may not be a good idea to put clay-filled clothes in your washing machine, unless you have access to an industrial laundry.

Reference: Jengo, 1995

72. Corys Brook Vesicular Basalt and Potential Carnelian

Vesicular basalt is common along Corys Brook.

County: Somerset
Site type: Stream gravels
Land status: Warren Township
Material: Vesicular basalt, potentially carnelian agate
Host rock: Stream gravels derived from Early Jurassic Orange Mountain Basalt
Difficulty: Moderate
Family-friendly: Yes, but family members may quickly get impatient
Tools needed: Screen, small shovel, hammer
Special concerns: Carnelian is a potential find here, but many of the rocks appear barren. Uncertain if collecting is allowed at this site.
Special attractions: None
GPS parking: N40° 38' 22" / W74° 29' 52"

Corys Brook drains the same ridge as Stirling Brook, which is a known locality for carnelian.

Topographic quadrangles: Chatham and Bernardsville, NJ
Finding the site: From I-78, take exit 36 to King George Road and turn south. Continue 1.7 miles south on King George Road and turn left (east) onto Reinman Road. Continue 0.5 mile east, and turn right (north) onto Sawmill Road. Proceed north about 0.1 mile, and look for a turnoff into the woods on the left (west) side of Saw Mill Road. The parking area is very small, and it is one of the only areas not heavily posted against trespassing, as it is owned by Warren Township. Park and walk to Corys Brook, which is just to the west.

Rockhounding

This is an unusual site in that the rock types and area make it a potential site for carnelian agate. During a brief visit in May 2012, I was unable to find any carnelian, but I found lots of vesicular basalt. This is important, as the vesicles in basalt often become filled with secondary minerals such as calcite, zeolites, and quartz, and carnelian agate is another potential secondary mineral. The basalts that I found were easy to crack open, and I found some very minor calcite but no carnelian. Many of the basalts were quite weathered, and any minerals that were in the vesicles may have weathered out of the rock. I also screened some of the gravels and was unable to find any carnelian, but this does not mean the carnelian is absent. Corys Brook drains the same ridge as Stirling Brook, which is well known for its carnelian, so Corys Brook should also have carnelian.

The site is also one of the only sites in the area that I have found that is not clearly posted as private land, and that in itself makes it worth a visit. The land is posted with Warren Township Committee signs, which clearly state that hunting, fishing, and motorized vehicles are prohibited, but hiking, photography, and nature studies are allowed. It may be a matter of interpretation as to whether screening stream gravels for carnelian can be considered a "nature study," so if you do screen gravels at this site, be sure to fill in any digging holes and leave the area in better shape than it was when you arrived.

Sites 72–73

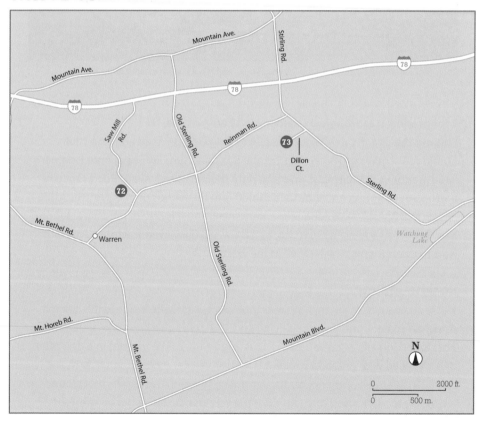

73. Stirling Brook Carnelian Agate

These carnelian pieces were found in about 10 minutes with a screen and small shovel.

See map page 220.
County: Somerset
Site type: Stream gravels
Land status: Private land, not posted
Material: Carnelian agate
Host rock: Stream gravels derived from Early Jurassic Orange Mountain basalt
Difficulty: Moderate
Family-friendly: Yes, but family members may quickly get impatient
Tools needed: Screen, small shovel, hammer
Special concerns: Area is heavily overworked
Special attractions: None
GPS parking: N40° 54' 21" / W74° 11' 10"
Topographic quadrangle: Chatham, NJ

Stirling Brook is very small and the stream bed is full of basalt.

Finding the site: From I-78, take exit 36 to King George Road and turn south. Continue 1.7 miles south on King George Road and turn left (east) onto Reinman Road. Continue 1.7 miles east to Stirling Road, and turn right (south). Continue on Stirling Road for approximately 0.1 mile, and turn right (west) onto Community Place. A small strip mall is here, and you can park at the southwestern end of the complex near the power lines. Stirling Brook is just south of the power lines. Hike to the brook, and the collecting area is all along the brook in the stream gravels.

Rockhounding

This is private property but the area was not posted during my visit in May 2012, and I did not experience any problems with parking at the strip mall. This site is well known for carnelian agate. You will need a screen and a small shovel to wash the stream gravels and look for carnelian. A screen is easily constructed with four pieces of wood that are screwed together, and a wire mesh screen with 0.3-inch or larger holes is then placed over the wood. I use duct tape on the screen to keep the sharp screws and screen edges from ripping my fingers.

This simple screen was made with small pine boards, inexpensive mesh screen, screws, and duct tape.

This site is quite worked over, and many previous carnelian hunters have dug several holes around the bank. This has given the area the appearance of a lunar landscape, but with trees. This is unfortunate as I am sure the landowner is very unhappy about all of these holes, so if you dig any holes, be sure to fill them before you leave the site. I focused on screening the gravels within the brook, and within a few screens found a small, bright piece of carnelian agate. However, you have to be patient. As anyone who has ever panned for gold can tell you, panning or screening sediments in a creek is hard work, but at least when panning for carnelian in Stirling Brook, you are likely to at least find some carnelian. Every bit of gravel has likely already been screened many times, but there is still the opportunity to find large pieces of carnelian that were missed. You may also want to consider hiking along the power line and entering Stirling Brook further to the west, as the sites nearest the parking area have undoubtedly seen the most collecting activity.

Reference: Stepanski and Snow, 2000

74. North Arlington Schuyler Copper Mine

Breaking open the rocks can reveal bright green copper mineralization.

County: Bergen

Site type: Mine dumps and outcrops on steep hillside

Land status: Private land, many sections are posted against trespassing, adjacent to industrial park and residential neighborhood

Material: Malachite, chrysocolla, azurite also reported

Host rock: Triassic-age Brunswick Formation shales

Difficulty: Moderately difficult

Family-friendly: No, hillside is very steep, access is difficult

Tools needed: Hammer, gloves, boots

Special concerns: Very small collecting area, very brushy, ticks, briars, area has lots of broken glass and sharp metal, boots, gloves, and long pants are required

Special attractions: New York City

GPS parking: N40° 46' 32" / W74° 07' 44"

GPS mine dumps: N40° 46' 34" / W74° 07' 45"

Topographic quadrangle: Central Park, NY-NJ

Finding the site: Take I-280 to Exit 16 to Harrison Avenue. Turn left (east) on to Harrison Avenue, and proceed 0.8 mile to Schuyler Avenue. Turn left (north), and take Schuyler Avenue 2.2 miles to the intersection with NJ 7, which is also known as the Belleville Turnpike. Turn right (southeast) on to the Belleville Turnpike, proceed about 0.1 mile, and take the fork to the left, which is Porete Avenue. The parking area to access the site is on the east side of Porete Avenue and just north of where Porete Avenue turns east into an industrial park. Park here and take the small trail that leads into the woods. The trail quickly drops off a very steep grade, and outcrops of malachite-stained sediments are present in this area. Climb along the hillside to the east and you will then encounter the mine dumps.

Rockhounding

The Schuyler copper mine is one of the oldest mines in the United States. Operations began around 1715, and the mine was operated periodically during the eighteenth and nineteenth centuries. The underground workings were considerable, but after the Civil War, mining had almost entirely stopped. Some attempts were made to restart the mine during the end of the nineteenth and early twentieth centuries, but these were not successful. The mine is now all but entirely covered by residential and industrial development, but the outcrops and dumps aboveground still produce copper minerals.

This is a very tricky area to access. I was able to reach the outcrops and dumps without crossing any NO TRESPASSING signs, but the indistinct paths along the hillside take you very close to the industrial properties along Porete Avenue, and all of these are clearly posted. Many of these are also inactive industrial properties that are undoubtedly patrolled, so you have to be careful that you are not inadvertently accessing posted ground. The hillside with the dumps is so brushy and trash filled that I was unable to move much further east, but there were obviously many more sections with copper minerals as you moved east along the steep hillside.

The outcrops are stained in sections with green mineralization that appeared to be largely malachite, but chrysocolla and azurite are also reported at this locality. The best way to find the copper mineralization is to look for obvious staining and break open the rocks. Many of the rocks have very bright green mineralization on freshly broken surfaces. You absolutely must have good boots,

Sites 74–78

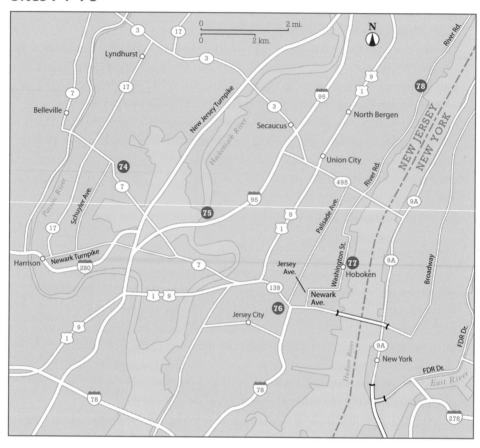

gloves, and long pants for this site, as much of the trash includes broken glass, boards with nails, and sharp metal, and this is not a good place for anyone who is looking for an easy place to see copper mineralization. There may also be better areas to access this site, but I was not able to easily find any other places that were not obviously posted against trespassing.

References: Stepanski and Snow, 2000; Woodward, 1944

75. Snake Hill Magnetite, Malachite, and Stilbite

Malachite is commonly found on the ground just west of the fence on the east side of the former workings.

See map page 226.
County: Hudson
Site type: Former quarry
Land status: Hudson County Park, collecting not allowed
Material: Stilbite, malachite, magnetite
Host rock: Jurassic diabase
Difficulty: Easy to moderately difficult
Family-friendly: Yes, excellent parking, much of area flat
Tools needed: None, collecting likely not allowed
Special concerns: Rubble along unfenced quarry walls is difficult to traverse
Special attractions: Field Station: Dinosaurs, located at Laurel Hill Park
GPS parking: N40° 45' 33" / W74° 5' 18"

Snake Hill is the high point next to the highway bridge.

Topographic quadrangle: Weehawken, NJ-NY
Finding the site: Take I-95 (New Jersey Turnpike) to exit 15X, follow the road south, and it will turn back north in a very tight loop. Follow this road north to where it passes under the turnpike, and take the third left (west), which is New County Road. The distance from Exit 15X to New County Road is approximately 2.1 miles. Take New County road approximately 1 mile into Laurel Hill Park and park in the parking area nearest the former quarry highwall.

Rockhounding

Snake Hill would have been an outstanding site to visit when it was quarried, but it is now a county park. It has excellent parking, and some of the area is still accessible for looking at rocks. This site is undoubtedly known to many commuters along I-95 as the prominent graffiti-covered hill on the north side of the highway that resembles the mountain on the Prudential Financial logo. Most of the former quarry walls are fenced off and are off-limits, but there is an unfenced area on the west end of the former quarry that has a great deal of rocks that you can look at closely. Many of these rocks have small veins of white stilbite,

Distinct magnetite crystals can be found in the low hills of the north end of the workings.

which occurs as small radiating crystals on the surface of the diabase. The east and north sides of the quarry are fenced, but just east of the parking area is an area with a lot of loose rock on the ground, some of which has the distinct bright green of malachite. Slightly further to the north are some unfenced rock outcrops, and some of these have rocks with octahedral magnetite crystals.

In late May 2012, Field Station: Dinosaurs opened at Laurel Hill Park. Field Station: Dinosaurs is an animatronic dinosaur park with more than thirty dinosaurs, and it is located very close to the areas described at this site. I have not yet been to this exhibit, so I am not sure how this affects looking at the rocks, but it may have shut off access to many of the areas described in this listing. If you visit this site, you may consider taking a tour of Dinosaurs, and I recommend advance planning as the exhibit often sells out, based on information from their website.

References: Darton, 1908; Peacor and Dunn, 1982; Puffer and Peters, 1974

76. Jersey City Bergen Arches Calcite

The calcite from outside of the Erie tunnel has a unique pattern of lamellae that is easily visible in hand samples.

See map page 226.
County: Hudson
Site type: Railroad cuts
Land status: Railroad and city property, not posted, sections likely not legal to access
Material: Calcite, minor pyrite, some igneous rocks
Host rock: Jurassic diabase
Difficulty: Moderate
Family-friendly: No, active rail line at Erie tunnel, homeless people live under arches
Tools needed: Hammer, chisel
Special concerns: Unusual characters under the highway and arches, railroad property

The Bergen Tunnel is a key landmark to find the Bergen Arches, as the Arches are immediately to the south, or to the left, of this view of the tunnel.

Special attractions: Jersey City and New York City
GPS west end of 8th Street (area for approaching site): N40° 43' 40" / W74° 3' 8"
GPS Bergen Tunnel Cut (calcite, pyrite, and other minerals): N40° 44' 53" / W74° 03' 9"
GPS southeast end of Bergen Arches (first arch): N40° 43' 53" / W74° 3' 11"
GPS northwest end of Bergen Arches (last arch, next to Erie Tunnel): N40° 44' 23" / W74° 3' 44"
Topographic quadrangle: Jersey City, NJ
Finding the site: This site can be very tricky to find and is best located using aerial photographs and walking to the site. Take I-78 or NJ 139, also known as the Pulaski Skyway, toward the Holland Tunnel, and turn south on Marin Boulevard just before you enter the tunnel. Continue south approximately 0.1 mile, and look for parking in this area. I recommend parking at the nearby Newport Mall or in paid parking lots of the hotels along the waterfront and walking to the site. Make sure you park in a legal space, as you do not want to get a ticket or get your car towed. You must also be careful to park your car in a safe place, so a paid garage or parking lot is highly recommended. After I found parking (which in my case was

at the paid parking lot of a nearby hotel), I had to access the arches by crossing a path by Dickenson High School, which is right next to the arches, and I accessed the Bergen Tunnel Cut by walking under I-78.

Rockhounding

The Erie Railroad cut was a huge cut through the Jurassic diabase of the New Jersey Palisades that was built to connect trains from the main line of the Erie Railroad to the Hudson River waterfront in Jersey City. The route was made to accommodate four lines of track, and this eliminated the expensive and dangerous gridlock that previously resulted when trains either tried to leave or get into Jersey City. The cut and the associated arches were constructed from 1906 to 1910 and were a major engineering feat for their time. However, it was also a ruinously expensive feat, as the project led to financial troubles for the Erie Railroad.

The Bergen Arches, which are bridges for the streets that cross the cut, were not known as the Bergen Arches until the 1980s. The area was previously referred to as the Erie Railroad cut, and the name Bergen Arches did not appear until preservationists began using the name. Arches are apparently easier to preserve than railroad cuts. The area is currently being considered for either a new highway or rail line, and the need for preserving the area has become more pressing as more and more of Jersey City becomes redeveloped.

Collecting in the Erie Cut is extreme urban collecting. You have all of the dangerous aspects typical of an urban site, including homeless camps and active rail lines, and much of the manmade parts of the landscape are covered with graffiti. This is not a good site to bring your family, especially if you have small children. However, you can get a Starbucks coffee on your walk to the site, which you can rarely do anywhere else.

Calcite is the most interesting mineral I observed at this locality, and it is confined to the outcrops next to the Bergen Arches outside of the Bergen and Erie Tunnels. The Bergen Arches themselves cross over the Erie Railroad cut, and nearly all the track has been removed. The diabase is well exposed in the cut, but I was unable to find any good zones with zeolites or other interesting minerals. The cut is also filled with trash, heavy brush, and trees, so it is very hard to collect in the cut. I highly recommend steel-toed boots, gloves, and a powerful flashlight to walk through the cut. Some of the tunnels under the arches are quite long and you do not want to be surprised in the dark.

Reference: Manchester, 1919

77. Hoboken Serpentine

Some of the serpentine has a waxy luster and is a shade of light blue and green.

See map page 226.
County: Hudson
Site type: Cliffs along Frank Sinatra Drive
Land status: Private property, not posted
Material: Green and yellow serpentine
Host rock: Late Precambrian to Cambrian-age metamorphosed peridotite
Difficulty: Easy
Family-friendly: Yes, very scenic area with excellent access
Tools needed: None, collecting likely not allowed
Special concerns: Parking may be expensive during daytime
Special attractions: Hoboken and New York City
GPS pier on Frank Sinatra Drive: N40° 44' 44" / W74° 01' 21"
Topographic quadrangle: Jersey City, NJ

The serpentine outcrops are right next to Frank Sinatra Drive, and the area has an excellent view of Manhattan.

Finding the site: The roads and exits in northern New Jersey are perpetually under construction, so you should update your GPS or maps before going to this site. Take I-78 east into northern New Jersey and head toward New York City. Take exit 58B, which leads to US 1-9 North, which then becomes NJ 139 East. Turn left on Jersey Avenue, continue 0.4 mile, and bear right as the road turns into Newark Avenue. Continue 0.3 mile on Newark Avenue, and Newark Avenue then turns into Observer Highway. Continue east 0.4 mile on Observer Highway, and turn left (north) onto Washington Street. Continue on Washington Street 0.3 mile, and turn right on 3rd Street. Head east 0.2 mile toward the Hudson River, and turn left (north) onto Frank Sinatra Drive. Drive north on Frank Sinatra Drive for approximately 0.5 mile, and you will see the outcrops on the west side of Frank Sinatra Drive. The GPS coordinates provided will take you to a local pier next to the outcrops, and parking may be available along Frank Sinatra Drive. If street parking is not available, you may have to park at a nearby parking garage.

The serpentine cliffs are very near the sidewalk and are easy to view up close.

Rockhounding

This site offers an excellent opportunity to view serpentine outcrops in an urban setting with a spectacular view of New York City. From the south, the serpentine outcrops begin where the cliffs start, just north of Frank Sinatra Park, and continue northward until the cliffs stop just south of Elysian Park. A sidewalk parallels the outcrops, and you can see outcrops up close. The serpentine in this area is various shades of green and light blue, and varies from light yellow-green to light blue and bright green to dark green. Loose pieces of serpentine are also present in the grass and brush alongside the cliffs. The area is private property and thick with joggers and tourists, so collecting and hammering on the outcrops is not recommended. However, even if you do not collect any rocks, the site is well worth checking out as the exposures are outstanding.

References: Beard, 2011; Darton, 1882

78. North Bergen Banded Hornfels

The hornfels have distinct bands and are generally light to dark gray.

See map page 226.
County: Bergen
Site type: Base of cliff wall
Land status: Private land, not posted, adjacent to condominiums and townhomes
Material: Banded hornfels
Host rock: Triassic-age sediments of the Stockton Formation intruded by diabases of Palisades Sill
Difficulty: Easy
Family-friendly: No, too close to cliff wall and condominiums
Tools needed: None, collecting not allowed
Special concerns: Lots of brush, ticks, close to cliff wall
Special attractions: New York City
GPS parking: N40° 48' 13" / W73° 59' 39"
Topographic quadrangle: Central Park, NY-NJ

The hornfels can be seen in the cliff wall just off Churchill Road in North Bergen.

Finding the site: North Bergen is just south of the I-95 Bridge, which is also known as the George Washington Bridge. From I-95, take exit 73 south to Hudson Terrace, which turns into Main Street and then River Road. From I-95, continue approximately 4 miles, and turn west onto Churchill Road. Continue approximately 300 feet up Churchill Road, which begins a short climb toward the cliffs, and park on the right side of Churchill Road. From here you can easily see the cliffs with the banded hornfels.

Rockhounding

Hornfels are fine-grained rocks that have been contact-metamorphosed by high-temperature intrusive rocks at shallow depths. At this locality the hornfels formed in Triassic sediments of the Stockton Formation that were intruded by Early Jurassic diabases of the Palisades Sill. The hornfels along the cliff face have distinct alternating light- to dark-gray bands, which suggests that some of the original sediments may have been carbonaceous. Many loose pieces of hornfels lie in the flat area between the cliffs and Churchill Road, and these rocks are extremely hard and dense. The cliffs have been partially covered with a wire mesh screen to reduce the danger from falling rocks along the cliff, but it is still dangerous to be next to the cliff face as rocks can fall at any time. This locality offers an excellent opportunity to view the hornfels, but as it is private property, be aware that access can change at any time. Be sure that you do not disturb any of the residents of the area when you are looking at the rocks. Do not enter the property if it is posted.

Reference: Colbert, 1965

79. New Street Quarries and Great Falls of the Passaic

The Great Falls of the Passaic are one of the more impressive waterfalls in the northeastern United States.

County: Passaic
Site type: Former quarries and waterfall
Land status: Quarries on private land, can access Great Falls for viewing
Material: Zeolite minerals
Host rock: Lower Jurassic Orange Mountain basalt
Difficulty: Difficult, much of basalt is barren
Family-friendly: Yes, but only to see the falls and basalt, quarries inaccessible
Tools needed: None, collecting not allowed
Special concerns: Quarry highwalls, ticks
Special attractions: None
GPS parking, New Street quarries: N40° 54' 21" / W74° 11' 10"
GPS parking, Great Falls of the Passaic: N40° 55' 03" / W74° 10' 53"

The Upper New Street Quarry is capped by a residential development and posted against trespassing.

Topographic quadrangle: Paterson, NJ

Finding the site: To get to the New Street Quarries from I-80, take exit 56A to Squirrelwood Road, which turns into CR 636. Continue 0.4 mile on Squirrelwood Road, and turn left (north) on Rifle Camp Road, which turns into New Street. Continue approximately 0.4 mile, and you will soon see a large gate with a fence on the east side of New Street. This is the entrance to the former Upper New Street Quarry. The former Lower New Street Quarry is on the west side of New Street, just southwest of the upper quarry. A small parking area for a maximum of two cars is on the west side of New Street.

To get to the Great Falls, continue north on New Street, cross I-80, and turn right onto Grand Street. Continue on Grand Street for 0.3 mile to Spruce Street, and turn left (north). Follow Spruce Street 0.5 mile, which will take you across the Passaic River, and turn right (east) on Maple Street. Continue 0.1 mile on Maple Street, which then bends sharply to the north, and there is a small spur to Maple Street that turns southeast. Turn southeast onto this spur, and parking is available here. From here you can walk to viewing points of the Great Falls of the Passaic.

Site 79

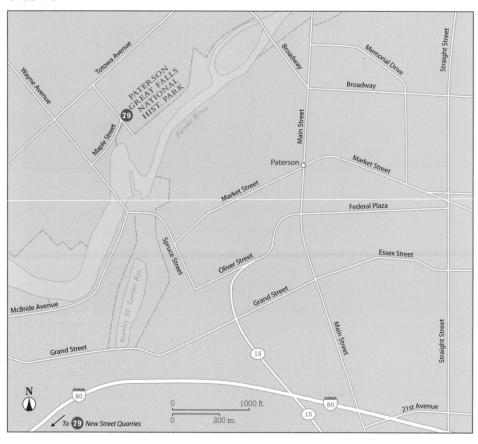

Rockhounding

The New Street Quarries are world famous localities for zeolite minerals, but they are private and off-limits unless you have permission for access. At the Lower New Street Quarry, you can access the basalt and edges of the quarry without crossing any NO TRESPASSING signs, but I found these sections of the basalt extremely barren. I did not get access to any sections of the Upper New Street Quarry, but I assume the sections that are not within the quarry are also barren of zeolite minerals. It appears likely that the best areas for collecting are off-limits without permission, and I understand that the properties are patrolled. Nevertheless, these are very important New Jersey localities, so they are listed in this book. Some colleges and local clubs occasionally offer field trips to the quarries, and this is by far the best way to get access for collecting.

The Great Falls of the Passaic are a worthwhile geologic stop when in the Paterson area. The falls are approximately 50 feet high, making this one of the highest waterfalls in the northeastern United States. The falls strongly influenced the industrial development of the Paterson region, as they were a ready source of hydropower for several local mills. Collecting is not allowed at the falls, but if you are visiting the New Street Quarries or otherwise in the Paterson area, it is well worth stopping by the falls for a brief visit.

Understanding the geology of the falls is also helpful to understanding where you are most likely to see zeolite minerals in the Paterson area. The falls formed in a fissure in the lower flow of the Early Jurassic Orange Mountain basalt near the contact with the underlying sediments of the Late Triassic Passaic Formation. This fissure was later carved into a chasm by the Passaic River, and glacial erosion removed the more easily erodible pillow lavas of the upper flows of the Orange Mountain basalt. The pillow lavas, which formed when the basalt was extruded and cooled quickly under the sea, had many gas pockets and fractures. Many of the zeolite minerals in the New Street Quarries and the other quarries of the area formed in these pillow lavas, so these are a key feature to look for if you have the opportunity to visit any of the quarries or basalt flows in the area. If you ever learn of a large construction project in the area, it may be worthwhile to check the rocks or exposures to see if they have zeolites, provided you can get permission for access.

Reference: Peters, 1984

80. Lake Valhalla Yellow Serpentine

The former quarry can be seen from the trail, but it is so overgrown that it can be missed if you are not looking for it.

County: Morris
Site type: Small former quarry
Land status: Morris County Park Commission property
Material: Yellow serpentine
Host rock: Franklin limestone
Difficulty: Easy
Family-friendly: Yes, excellent place for hiking and seeing rocks
Tools needed: None, collecting not allowed
Special concerns: Ticks, lots of bugs in undergrowth, bears
Special attractions: None
GPS parking: N40° 56' 15" / W74° 22' 34"
GPS quarry: N40° 56' 37" / W74° 22' 25"

GPS visitor center: N40° 56' 48" / W74° 23' 18"

Topographic quadrangles: Boonton and Pompton Plains, NJ

Finding the site: Take I-287 to Montville, which is exit 47, and head west for approximately 0.2 mile on US 202. Turn right (north) onto Valhalla Road, and go under a railroad, which is approximately 0.2 mile up the road. Continue another 0.4 mile, and the road is now called Vista Road. Turn right (north) onto Lake Shore Drive, and drive approximately 0.7 mile along the west side of Lake Valhalla. Lake Shore then crosses Hemlock Road. Cross Hemlock Road and continue about 400 feet to the end of Lake Shore Drive. Park on the side of the road. Walk past the house on the left and into the woods, and look for a trail. Walk up the trail, and in approximately ten minutes, you will come to an intersection with a trail that goes off to the left. Stay on the trail

This exposed yellow serpentine was broken off by previous visitors to the site.

to the right. Continue for another ten to fifteen minutes, and follow the trail as it goes up a ridge, and the quarry is to the right of the trail. At the time of my latest visit in 2012, the trail was marked as the "yellow" trail. An alternative way to reach the site is to park at the visitor center and follow their maps and the yellow trail to the "limestone quarry" they show on their maps.

Rockhounding

This quarry has been inactive for nearly 130 years as of 2012. The bedrock geology is described as Franklin limestone, and the origin of the serpentine may be due to alteration of the mineral diopside as a result of fluids from a pegmatite exposed in the quarry. Other minerals reported in the quarry include granular dolomite, chrysotile, picrolite, and phlogopite.

The quarry is well overgrown but it is very easy to walk through the area and see exposures with yellow serpentine on the rocks. The quarry walls are mainly

Sites 80–82

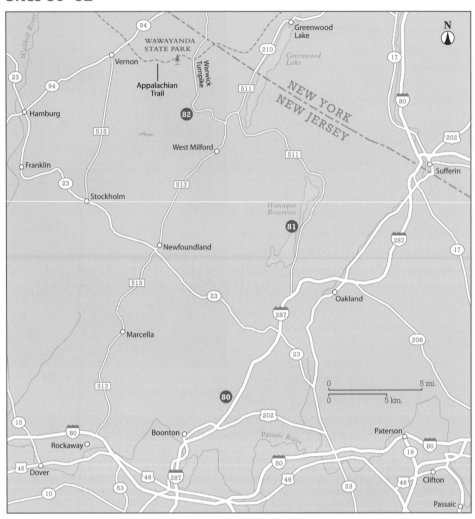

extremely hard gray crystalline rock of the Franklin limestone, smooth dark-green serpentine, and many veins and stringers of yellow serpentine. Rock collecting is not allowed in the park, but signs of rock hounds are everywhere, from broken rocks along the walls of the quarry to freshly broken samples of yellow serpentine on boulders on the quarry floor.

References: Beard, 2004; Shannon, 1927; Stepanski and Snow, 2000

81. Wanaque Roomy and Blue Mines Magnetite

The Roomy Mine is on the hillside on the north side of the orange trail.

See map page 244.

County: Passaic

Site type: Former 19th-century iron mines

Land status: Owned by New Jersey Audubon Society, Weis Ecology Center, no collecting allowed

Material: Magnetite

Host rock: Precambrian-age gneisses and amphibolites

Difficulty: Easy, magnetite is easy to identify in loose rocks on mine dumps

Family-friendly: Yes, excellent place for hiking and to see old mines

Tools needed: None, collecting not allowed

Special concerns: Trail may be strenuous for some

Special attractions: None

GPS Roomy Mine: N41° 03' 53" / W74° 18' 59"

The east Blue Mine is hard to find as it is off the trail, and it is on the east side of the ridge just south of the trail.

GPS East Blue Mine: N41° 03' 41" / W74° 18' 52"
GPS West Blue Mine: N41° 03' 35" / W74° 19' 03"
Topographic quadrangle: Wanaque, NJ
Finding the site: Take I-287 to exit 55, and proceed north through Wanaque on CR 511 for approximately 3.8 miles. Turn left (west) onto West Brook Road, proceed approximately 2 miles to Snake Den Road, and turn left (south). Continue on Snake Den Road for approximately 0.7 mile, and you will see a small parking area on the right. You can park here or continue up the road and park at the Weis Ecology Center. It is highly recommended that you stop here and get a *Norvin Green State Forest Trail Map,* as the mines are nearly impossible to find unless you know where to go on the trails.

At the time of my visit in April 2012, the trails were flagged by painting trees along the trail. You have to walk from the Weis Ecology Center past the Highlands Natural Pool and continue across a bridge that crosses a small creek. Watch the trees for the green squares. Follow this to a display for trail notices, and continue up the hill, watching now for the yellow/blue trail symbols on the trees. The trail is very indistinct in this area and by now you should be looking at your map.

Continue up the hill and turn left onto the yellow trail. Continue on yellow and turn left onto orange, and you will soon pass a small waterfall, which is Wyanokie Falls, on your right. Continue past the falls and you will see a large rock on the left. Turn right and then left and follow the trail to the Roomy Mine, which is on the left side of the trail on the hill.

To get to the Blue Mines, go back down the orange trail and turn south on the yellow/red trail, and continue on this trail until it ends at an east-west trail. To get to the east Blue Mine, follow the trail and look for a faint footpath up the hill to the south. Follow the path on this hill to the east, and it ends near a small cut that is filled with water. There is a mine dump adjacent to the cut. To get to the west Blue Mine, go back to the intersection of the yellow/red trail with the east-west trail, and the mine is just to the west of the trail intersection. The west Blue Mine is a cut with a deep pond in front. To return to the Weis Ecology Center, take the trail over a small bridge that crosses the creek, and proceed back to the center, which is about a forty-five-minute hike from the west Blue Mine. Bear in mind that while the trail map is useful, I found that it was rather inaccurate with respect to the trails and the creeks, so you must pay attention to the paint symbols on the trees to know which trails you are on.

Rockhounding

While collecting is not allowed, the area is well worth visiting to see the mines and observe the magnetite in outcrop and in the tailings dumps. The Roomy Mine was opened shortly after 1840 and was worked until about 1857, then briefly re-explored around 1890. The Blue Mine is older and was first discovered and opened around 1765. The Blue Mine was again worked during the early nineteenth century and reopened briefly a few times in 1871, 1886, and 1890. The tailings dumps at the Roomy Mine and the Blue Mine have lots of magnetite in outcrop and as loose pieces on the ground. The magnetite is easy to identify as it is dark gray to black, has a semimetallic luster, is extremely dense, and is strongly attracted to a magnet. Some of the magnetite in loose pieces and outcrop has small, reasonably well-formed octahedral crystal faces. I also noticed that some of the rocks in the stream near the Blue Mine are loaded with shiny phlogopite or biotite, and this actually shines in the water like bright gold. I am sure many visitors to this site probably thought they saw gold in the creek when they first came to these mines.

Reference: Lenik, 1996

82. West Milford–Bearfort Mountain Puddingstone

The puddingstone, formally the Skennemunk Conglomerate, has large white quartz pebbles in a light purplish-brown matrix.

See map page 244.
County: Passaic
Site type: Outcrops and loose rocks
Land status: Abram S. Hewitt State Forest, no collecting allowed
Material: Puddingstone, a light-purplish-brown conglomerate with white quartz pebbles
Host rock: Late Devonian-age Skunnemunk conglomerate
Difficulty: Easy, virtually the entire mountain is puddingstone
Family-friendly: Yes, excellent place for hiking and seeing rocks
Tools needed: None, collecting not allowed
Special concerns: Ticks, parking along roadcuts
Special attractions: None

The puddingstone can be seen in outcrops throughout the mountainside and is easily reached from the parking area.

GPS parking: N41° 9' 59" / W74° 22' 44.5"

Topographic quadrangle: Wawayanda, NJ-NY

Finding the site: Starting in West Milford, take SR 513 approximately 1.8 miles north to Warwick Turnpike. Turn left (west) on Warwick Turnpike, and you will then proceed up the hill. Roadcuts of puddingstone are all along the turnpike as you cross over Bearfort Mountain, and the area to the north is Abram S. Hewitt State Forest. However, this road is very busy and you may find it difficult to find safe parking to look at these roadcuts. I suggest proceeding an additional 1.8 miles to the intersection with Lake Shore Drive, turning right (north), and parking in the first pull-off on the east side of Lake Shore Drive immediately north of this intersection.

Rockhounding

Bearfort Mountain is well known as a locality for New Jersey puddingstone, which is a light-purplish-brown conglomerate with white quartz pebbles. This locality is on the west flank of Bearfort Mountain, and it offers an easy-to-reach and safe location to see the puddingstone. It is an attractive rock and is an interesting example of a conglomerate with large pebbles in a finer-grained matrix. Although collecting is not allowed, as a state forest, it is easy to access and look at the rocks.

83. Cranberry Lake Iron Mines

Look for this sign on the Sussex Branch Trail, as it indicates where to take the trail for the iron mine.

County: Sussex
Site type: Mine dumps
Land status: Allamuchy State Park
Material: Magnetite and associated minerals
Host rock: Precambrian granitic and pyroxenitic gneisses
Difficulty: Moderate
Family-friendly: Yes
Tools needed: None, collecting not allowed
Special concerns: Very easy to get lost on trails, very helpful to have maps
Special attractions: None
GPS parking: N40° 56' 52" / W74° 44' 15"
GPS IRON MINE TRAIL sign: N40° 56' 21" / W74° 44' 24"
GPS Iron mine adit: N40° 56' 31" / W74° 44' 38"

Sites 83–86

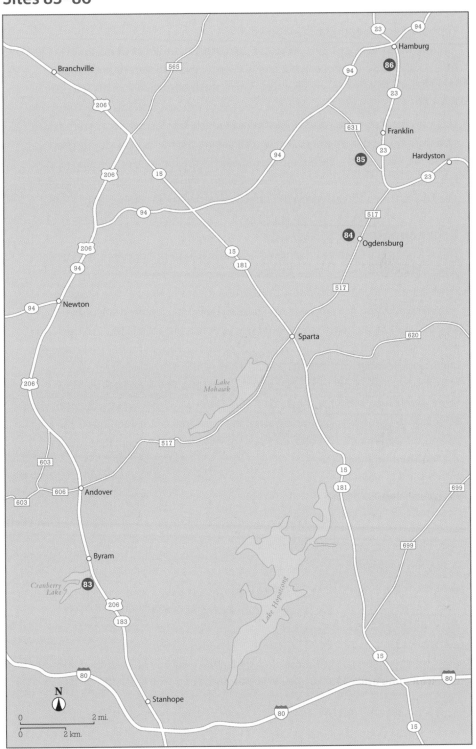

Branchville
565
206

23 94
Hamburg
94 86
23
631 Franklin
23
Hardyston
85
23

94
206 15
517
94
84 Ogdensburg
206 15
94 181 517
Newton
94
Sparta 620
206
Lake Mohawk
517
15
181
603
606 Andover
603
699
699
Byram
Cranberry Lake 83
206 Lake Hopatcong
183
80
N
0   2 mi.
0   2 km.
Stanhope
80
80 15

GPS Prospect pit: N40° 56' 26" / W74° 44' 30"

Topographic quadrangle: Stanhope, NJ

Finding the site: From I-80, take exit 25 to north US 206. Proceed north on US 206 for 3.6 miles to South Shore Road, and turn left (west). Proceed southwest on South Shore Road for approximately 0.4 mile and look for a fork to the left. Take this fork to the parking area, which is the start of the Sussex Branch Trail. This trail occupies the former rail route of old Sussex Branch Railroad, which operated from 1848 to 1966. Approximately 0.8 mile south along the trail is a sign for the Iron Mine Trail, and a small caved mine is right next to the trail sign on the side of the hill. Take the trail into the hills and it will lead to a short adit for an iron mine, and a side trail to the southeast along the ridge will lead to small prospect pit.

Rockhounding

This is a great site to visit as the hiking is relatively easy, but since this is a state park, no rock collecting is allowed. However, you can still see many minerals in mine dumps and loose rocks near caved mines near the IRON MINE TRAIL sign, the iron-mine adit, and the prospect pit. The area is also the reported site of the BEMCO uranium rare-earth mine, but I was unable to find the BEMCO mine during my visit to the area as I had apparently not taken the correct trail. Since I could not confirm the location of the BEMCO mine, I have left it off the locality map.

It is very easy to get lost on these trails, and I strongly suggest bringing a topographic map and a hand-held GPS unit. There is another sign for the Iron Mine Trail to the south, and this is part of the same trail, but it definitely is the long way to the iron-mine adit. I suggest sticking with the first trail sign that you see to get to the iron-mine adit.

Reference: Vassiliou, 1980

84. Sterling Hill Mine and Mine Run Dump

Many of the original buildings and structures were preserved at the Sterling Hill Mining Museum.

See map page 251.

County: Sussex

Site type: Mine tour and mine run dump

Land status: Private land, fee collecting

Material: Franklinite, zincite, willemite, calcite, and several other minerals

Host rock: Franklin limestone

Difficulty: Easy

Family-friendly: Yes

Tools needed: Hammer, chisel, shortwave UV light if available

Special concerns: Bring collecting tools and a shortwave UV light

Special attractions: Nearby Franklin Mineral Museum

GPS parking: N41° 04' 59" / W74° 36' 12"

Topographic quadrangle: Franklin, NJ

Finding the site: Take CR 517 to Ogdensburg. In Ogdensburg, at Brooks Flat Road, there is a brown sign for the Sterling Hill Mining Museum on the west side of the road. Turn west here. Proceed down the hill for 0.4 mile and turn right (north) on Plant Street. Follow Plant Street 0.9 mile to the stop sign and turn left (west), then immediately left (south) again into the Sterling Hill Mining Museum entrance. The address is 30 Plant St., Ogdensburg, NJ 07439.

Rockhounding

New Jersey has no shortage of former industrial sites, and most of them have been obliterated during redevelopment, become permanently closed eyesores, or were turned into hazardous waste dumps and Superfund sites. The Sterling Hill Mine could have easily met the same fate. The mine closed in 1986 due to low zinc prices and a property tax dispute with the Borough of Ogdensburg. The mine was purchased in 1989 at a public auction by Richard and Robert Hauck, who transformed the mine site into a museum. The Sterling Hill Mining Museum opened for tours on August 4, 1990, and is now visited by more than 40,000 people annually.

No mineral collecting trip to northern New Jersey is complete without a visit to the Sterling Hill Mining Museum. As an added attraction, the museum offers fee collecting on their mine run dump. This dump is full of franklinite, calcite, willemite, and zincite and is an excellent opportunity to collect some very good specimens that came right from the mine. You should bring a short-wave ultraviolet (UV) light, a rock hammer, leather gloves, and safety glasses. Most of the pieces in the mine run dump are already relatively small so you should not need a sledgehammer. You have to pay by the pound for material that you take out, in addition to the collecting fee. The zinc minerals have a very high specific gravity, and the cost can add up quickly when you are paying by the pound.

References: Palache, 1935; Stepanski and Snow, 2000

85. Buckwheat Dump and Franklin Mineral Museum

The Buckwheat Dump can be accessed for collecting through the Franklin Mineral Museum.

See map page 251.
County: Sussex
Site type: Mine dump
Land status: Private land, fee collecting
Material: Franklinite, zincite, willemite, calcite, biotite, and several other minerals
Host rock: Franklin limestone
Difficulty: Easy
Family-friendly: Yes
Tools needed: Hammer, chisel, shortwave UV light if available
Special concerns: Bring collecting tools and a shortwave UV light
Special attractions: Nearby Sterling Hill Mining Museum
GPS parking: N41° 06' 48" / W74° 35' 18"
Topographic quadrangle: Franklin, NJ

Finding the site: Take NJ 23 to Franklin. Turn west onto CR 631, also known as Franklin Avenue. Continue 0.5 mile and turn right (north) onto Buckwheat Avenue. Continue about 0.1 mile, and take the first left (west) onto Evans Street. The Franklin Mineral Museum, which will provide fee access to the Buckwheat Dump, is on the south side of the road at 32 Evans St. in Franklin.

Rockhounding

One of the most frustrating aspects of visiting some mining towns and famous mineral localities is that while there may be lots of old buildings and displays about mining and minerals, you rarely have a place that is safe and legal for rock collecting. The owners of the Buckwheat Dump have addressed that issue in Franklin. The Buckwheat Dump is a very large waste-rock pile from zinc-mining operations at the nearby former mines, which closed by 1954.

I have collected on the Buckwheat Dump through field trips with regional mineral clubs. The Buckwheat Dump covers a very wide area, and it is well worth a collecting stop if you are looking to see good examples of some of the available minerals from the Franklin area. Much of the dump is waste rock that was not heavily mineralized with zinc, but you can still easily find lots of fluorescent minerals such as calcite and willemite, as well interesting nonfluorescent minerals such as franklinite, zincite, magnetite, and biotite. You should bring a short-wave ultraviolet (UV) light, a rock hammer, sledgehammer, chisel, leather gloves, and safety glasses. The UV light is a really good idea unless you are with a club that is providing lights. You have to pay by the pound for material that you take out, in addition to the collecting fee, and you will want to make sure you get the best fluorescent minerals. The dump has an amazing variety of minerals, and it is very easy to collect many heavy specimens with fantastic minerals, only to find that not many of them are fluorescent.

The Franklin Mineral Museum, which was started in 1964, has several thousand local and worldwide minerals on display. The museum has a very large fluorescent mineral display featuring minerals from the Franklin area as well as from around the world. I have not personally visited the museum, but I am sure it is well worth a visit for anyone interested in fluorescent minerals.

References: Palache, 1935; Stepanski and Snow, 2000

86. Hamburg Stromatolites

The stromatolite exposure is right next to a sidewalk and is easily accessible for viewing.

See map page 251.
County: Sussex
Site type: Outcrop
Land status: Private land, no collecting or hammering allowed
Material: Stromatolites
Host rock: Lower Ordovician–Upper Cambrian Allentown dolomite
Difficulty: Easy
Family-friendly: Yes
Tools needed: None, no collecting allowed
Special concerns: No collecting or hammering allowed, steep slopes on outcrop
Special attractions: Gingerbread Castle (now closed, can only view from road)
GPS parking: N41° 08' 35" / W74° 34' 41"
Topographic quadrangle: Hamburg, NJ

Finding the site: Take NJ 23 to Hamburg. Just south of the intersection of NJ 23 and NJ 94 is a railroad bridge, and just north of this bridge, Gingerbread Castle Road intersects the west side of NJ 23. Proceed west on Gingerbread Castle Road, approximately 0.3 mile, turn left (south) on Wheatsworth Road, and proceed into a housing development. Follow the road to the south as it circles in a broad bend, and after approximately 1,500 feet you will see a large, long, gray outcrop on the north side of the road. Drive toward the clubhouse for the development and park near the outcrop. The best stromatolite exposures are on the northwest side of the north end of the outcrop.

Rockhounding

Stromatolites are best described as fossilized algae. They formed as layers of algae built upon each other, and sedimentary grains and debris got caught in the algae mats and subsequently formed multiple layers that became accreted together. Stromatolites are among the oldest fossils on earth and were a major component of the fossil record for the first 3.5 billion years of life on Earth. They peaked in abundance about 1.25 billion years ago, and by the start of the Cambrian period, about 542 million years ago, they declined by about 30 percent. The reason for the decline was almost certainly the new abundance of plant-eating animals that evolved.

This outcrop shows the circular patterns formed by the stromatolites when exposed on flat surfaces. The outcrop is very smooth and was polished by glaciers when they covered this area, and distinct glacial striations can easily be seen along the entire outcrop. Nearly all of the striations parallel the overall shape of the outcrop, indicating glacial migration in a northeast–southwest direction. This exposure is only for looking and touching, not hammering or collecting. Please be sure to respect this outcrop, as it is on private property. The owners have graciously been allowing people to look at it closely, but this can change at any time.

As you leave the site, look toward the south as you turn right onto Gingerbread Castle Road. You will be able to see the Gingerbread Castle on the south side of the road adjacent to an abandoned mill. This was formerly a children's amusement park, but it closed in 2007 and has since fallen into disrepair. The castle is closed to visitors and clearly posted against trespassing, but it still is worth observing when you pass it on the road.

Reference: Schwimmer, 2012

87. Marble Mountain Hematite Mine

The main iron mineralization at the Marble Mountain mine is fine grained hematite, which often stains the rocks red.

County: Warren
Site type: Former iron mine
Land status: Marble Mountain Natural Resource Area
Material: Finely disseminated hematite
Host rock: Precambrian-age quartzite and shales
Difficulty: Easy
Family-friendly: Yes, hiking trail is relatively moderate
Tools needed: None, collecting may not be allowed
Special concerns: Traffic along River Road
Special attractions: Delaware River
GPS parking: N40° 42' 42" / W75° 11' 37"
GPS mine site: N40° 42' 54" / W75° 11' 18"
Topographic quadrangle: Easton, PA-NJ
Finding the site: This can be a tricky area to reach and your route depends on how you approach Phillipsburg, New Jersey. If you are coming from the west,

The mine is on the northwest flank of the southwestern end of Marble Mountain, just east of the Delaware River.

Take US 22 to Phillipsburg, New Jersey, and take the exit to get to Broad Street, which is the first exit after you cross the Delaware River. Proceed 0.9 mile north on Broad Street and turn right (east) on Fifth Street, proceed 0.1 mile, and turn north onto CR 621, aka River Road. The road will soon make a broad turn to the left (northwest), and you will see a gate on the west side of the road. A small metal sign that reads Marble Hill Natural Recreation Area is located near the gate. Parking is available near this gate, on the west side of River Road, but be sure that you do not block the gate, as beyond this is private property. The parking area is approximately 0.6 mile north of the intersection of CR 621 and Fifth Street.

If you are approaching Phillipsburg from the east, take the exit for Main Street and proceed north on North Main Street approximately 0.5 mile to the intersection with North Main and Fifth Street. North Main Street is CR 621/River Road at this point. Follow the directions above to reach the parking area from this intersection.

The trailhead to the site begins on the east side of the road and is nearly opposite the parking area. The trail leads diagonally up the northwest flank of the mountain, and it is marked by blue paint in the trees. Follow the trail approximately 0.3 mile to a fork in the trail, and take the trail to the right, which is marked with orange paint on the trees. The orange trail leads directly to the mine.

Rockhounding

This mine is also known as Fulmer's Mine, and it is sometimes also referred to as the Ice Cave, as apparently a great deal of ice gets inside the mine during the winter. The main iron ore mineral was hematite. The mine was reportedly first opened in 1860 and was only worked for a short period of time. The mine was re-explored in 1880 and 1886 but did not have enough iron ore to become economic. The principal mine workings consist of a large opening in the side of the mountain. The rocks outside of the mine have some minor hematite mineralization, and this generally consists of reddish staining and finely disseminated specular hematite. Many of the rocks have a silvery appearance and are very dense, and this also helps in identifying pieces with iron minerals at this site. Since this is part of the Marble Mountain Natural Resource Area, collecting is likely prohibited, but I did not see any signs that summarized the regulations for the area.

References: Bayley, 1910

Site 87

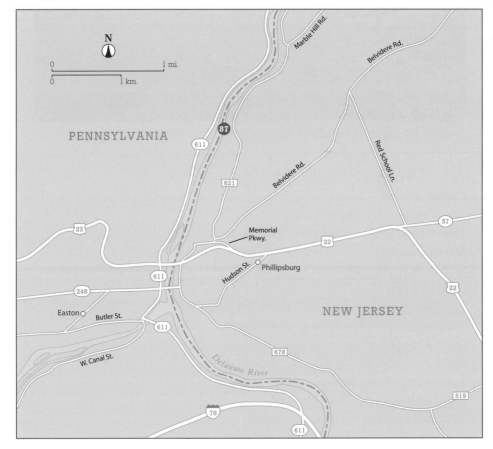

88. Pahaquarry Copper Mines

The upper workings are in a very broad cut on the west flank of the mountain.

County: Warren
Site type: Former copper mines
Land status: Delaware Water Gap National Recreation Area
Material: Copper minerals, mainly malachite, reported chalcocite
Host rock: Reddish siltstones and sandstones of Silurian Bloomsburg Formation
Difficulty: Easy
Family-friendly: Yes, excellent place for a day hike
Tools needed: None, collecting not allowed
Special concerns: Hike to the upper workings is very strenuous, no collecting allowed
Special attractions: Delaware River
GPS parking: N41° 02' 16" / W75° 01' 42"
GPS large adit: N41° 02' 08" / W75° 01' 33"

Traces of light green copper minerals can still be seen outside of the small adit, but collecting is not allowed at this site.

GPS small adit: N41° 02' 06" / W75° 01' 34"
GPS upper workings: N41° 01' 59" / W75° 01' 41"
Topographic quadrangle: Bushkill, PA-NJ
Finding the site: Take I-80 to exit 1, which is the exit near the New Jersey–Pennsylvania border. Proceed west on River Road, which soon turns north and becomes Old Mine Road, which is also known as CR 606. Note that this road is subject to seasonal closures and may be closed in the winter. Continue on Old Mine Road approximately 8 miles to the parking area to hike to the mines. The parking area is marked with a sign that reads COPPER MINES TRAIL PARKING AREA. Park here and follow the trails to the mines. To get to the larger adit, take the fork to the left; to get to the smaller adit, take the fork to the right. To get to the upper workings, take the fork to the right, then take the steep trail to the right to the first large shoulder along the ridge.

Rockhounding

This site is strictly for hiking and observing the mines, as no rock collecting is allowed within the Delaware Water Gap Recreation Area. The Pahaquarry copper mines are some of the oldest mine workings in North America. Mining started in the 1750s but was unsuccessful and ended by 1760. Attempts were made to open the mines again in the mid-1800s and early 1900s, but these also failed. During the last attempts in the early 1900s, a very large mill was constructed, but the ores did not have enough copper to be economic. The mines were abandoned shortly afterward, and the last of the equipment was removed by 1928.

Sites 88–89

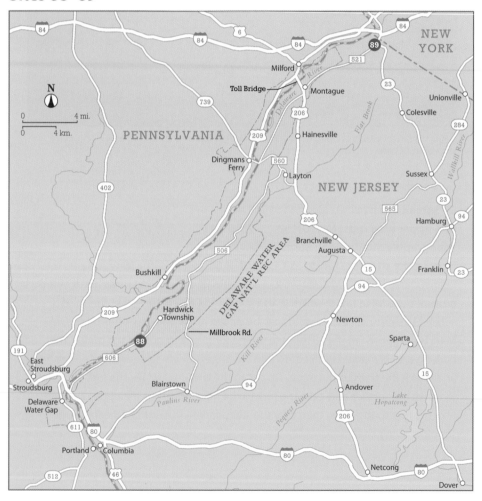

The trails lead to two adits along a small, steep brook with several small waterfalls, and the upper workings are in a very broad cut along the strike of northwest dipping beds of the Bloomsburg Formation. A minor amount of malachite can be found on the dumps of the small adit, which is the one that is farthest uphill from the creek. The large adit is close to the creek, and practically no mineralized dump material is left at this mine. A minor amount of malachite can also be found in the upper workings. Rock collecting is not allowed, which for this site is critical as the few remaining mineralized rocks are scarce, and the dumps could easily be picked clean. The mine adits, while you can see them, are also gated up to keep people out, as the bat population is threatened by white-nose syndrome, and minimizing bat contact with humans may help reduce the spread of this deadly bat disease.

Reference: Woodward, 1944

89. Montague Quartz Crystals

The crystals occur in veins and are generally small but relatively clear.

See map page 264.
County: Sussex
Site type: Outcrop
Land status: Uncertain, may be owned by Nature Conservancy
Material: Quartz crystals
Host rock: Siltstone and silty shale of the Lower Devonian Esopus Formation
Difficulty: Easy
Family-friendly: Yes
Tools needed: Hammer, chisel, gloves
Special concerns: Quartz veins located on steep hillside, snakes, ticks
Special attractions: Delaware Water Gap National Recreation Area
GPS trailhead: N41° 21' 07" / W74° 41' 33"
GPS quartz crystals: N41° 20' 53" / W74° 32' 11"

Topographic quadrangle: Port Jervis South, NY

Finding the site: From I-84 in New York, take exit 1 NJ 23, and head south on NJ 23. If already in northern New Jersey, take NJ 23 toward NJ 84 and the New York state line. Parking is available in the parking lot of the large shopping center approximately 0.1 mile south of the New York state line. Try to purchase lunch or other items from some of the businesses in this complex if you use their parking lot. If you patronize any of the other local businesses nearby, you may also be able to park at their establishments. From your parking area, walk across NJ 23 to the bridge that crosses Mill Creek. The trailhead to the quartz crystals is right next to the bridge. This trail roughly parallels Mill Creek and reportedly was the former highway before the current NJ 23 was constructed. From the trailhead, hike approximately 0.4 mile upstream (southwest). The valley widens in this area and the stream becomes a meandering stream in a wide, broad valley. To the right is a very steep path that leads to the outcrop with the quartz crystals.

Rockhounding

The quartz crystals occur in veins in the Lower Devonian Esopus Formation, which is a light- to dark-gray siltstone and silty shale. The quartz crystals occur in quartz veins with small vugs at a light-gray outcrop on the side of the ridge. Many loose rocks with crystals can be found at the base of the ridge below the outcrop if you do not want to climb to the outcrop. However, after coming this far it is a shame if you do not make the climb up the rocky slope to the outcrop. There are several small workings along the outcrop where the quartz veins intersect the surface.

The site is next to a sign that indicates that the land, at least by the swamp, is a nature preserve owned by the Nature Conservancy, NJ Skylands Program. ATVs and motor vehicles are prohibited, as are camping, hunting, fishing, trapping, and fires, and the removal or destruction of plants and wildlife is also prohibited. There are no signs specifically ruling out mineral collecting, but be aware that the status of this site can change at any time.

You must also be very careful to avoid snakes at this site. I saw several snakes among the rocks and one large snakeskin shed from molting. None of the snakes I saw were rattlesnakes, but rattlesnakes do occur in this region, so be careful here and at any other wooded sites with lots of rocks for hiding snakes, especially where the slopes face south and get warm during the day.

Reference: Drake et al., 1996

REFERENCES CITED

Arndt, H. H. *Geologic Map of the Ashland Quadrangle, Columbia and Schuylkill Counties, Pennsylvania.* US Geological Survey Geologic Quadrangle Map GQ-918, 1971.

Bartholomew, Craig L., and Lance E. Metz. *The Anthracite Iron Industry of the Lehigh Valley.* Center for Canal History and Technology, Phillipsburg, NJ: Harmony Press: 1988.

Bayley, William S. *Iron Mines and Mining in New Jersey.* Vol. VII of the Final Report Series of the State Geologist, 1910.

Beard, Robert. *Cabbage Head Quartz: Rosettes from Central Pennsylvania. Rock & Gem Magazine,* Nov. 2006, vol. 36, no. 11.

———. *Cape May Diamonds: Quartz Collecting in New Jersey. Rock & Gem Magazine,* March 2002, vol. 32, no. 3.

———. *Erie Horseshoe Crab Fossils: Pennsylvania's Best-Kept Collecting Secret. Rock & Gem Magazine,* June 2006, vol. 36, no. 6.

———. *Fruitville Pike Pseudomorphs: A Family-friendly Excursion in Lancaster County, Pennsylvania. Rock & Gem Magazine,* Nov. 2002, vol. 32, no. 11.

———. *Hay Creek Prehnite and Zeolites: Specimens South of Birdsboro, Pennsylvania. Rock & Gem Magazine,* Nov. 2008, vol. 38, no. 11.

———. *Hershey Hematite, Hematite, Garnets, and Chocolate in South-Central Pennsylvania. Rock & Gem Magazine,* Dec. 2006, vol. 36, no. 12.

———. *Hoboken Serpentine: Urban Outcrops Along the Hudson River. Rock & Gem Magazine,* June 2011, vol. 41, no. 6.

———. *Lake Valhalla Serpentine: This Is Serpentine of an Unusual Color. Rock & Gem Magazine,* Sept. 2004, vol. 34, no. 9.

———. *Oreland Goethite: A Family-Friendly Collecting Site Near Philadelphia. Rock & Gem Magazine,* Dec. 2004, vol. 34, no. 12.

———. *Pennsylvania Turquoise: A Blue-Green Surprise at Waggoner's Gap. Rock & Gem Magazine,* Dec. 2007, vol. 37, no. 12.

———. *Phoenixville Dolomite Crystals: A Unique Collecting Site Near Philadelphia. Rock & Gem Magazine,* Aug. 2007, vol. 37, no. 8.

————. *Prospect Park Kyanite: Rock Collecting in Urban Philadelphia.* Rock & Gem Magazine, Nov. 2001, vol. 31, no. 11.

————. *Reading Banks Bombshells: A Family-friendly Field Trip in Pennsylvania.* Rock & Gem Magazine, Feb. 2006, vol. 36, no. 2.

————. *Venango County Siderite Nodules: Collecting Iron Carbonate Crystals in Pennsylvania's Oil Country.* Rock & Gem Magazine, Aug. 2006, vol. 36, no. 8.

Beerbower, J. R. *Paleoecology of the Centerfield Coral Zone, East Stroudsburg Locality, Monroe County, Pennsylvania.* Pennsylvania Academy of Science Proceedings, 1957, vol. 31.

Blackmer, Gale C. *Bedrock Geologic Map of the Quarryville and Conestoga Quadrangles, Lancaster County, Pennsylvania.* Open File Report OFBM 07-03.0, Pennsylvania Geological Survey, Harrisburg, 2007.

Busch, Richard M., and Michael S. Fedosh. Welleraspis *(Trilobita) in the Conococheague Formation of Southeast Pennsylvania.* Pennsylvania Geology, Dec. 1978, vol. 9, no. 6.

Butts, Charles, and E. S. Moore. *Geology and Mineral Resources of the Bellefonte Quadrangle, Pennsylvania.* US Geological Survey Bulletin 855, 1936.

Caster, K. E., *Siliceous Sponges from the Mississippian and Devonian Strata of the Penn-York Embayment.* Journal of Paleontology, Jan. 1939, vol. 13, no. 1.

————. *The Stratigraphy and Paleontology of Northwestern Pennsylvania.* Bulletins of American Paleontology, 1934, vol. 21, no. 71.

Chapman, Randolph. *Contact-Metamorphic Effects of Triassic Diabase at Safe Harbor, Pennsylvania.* Geological Society of America Bulletin, 1950, vol. 61, no. 3., pp. 191–220.

Colbert, Edwin H. *A Phytosaur from North Bergen, New Jersey.* American Museum Motivates, American Museum of Natural History, no. 2230, September 10, 1965.

Darton, N. H. *The mineralogical localities in and around New York City, and the minerals occurring therein.* Scientific American Supplement, 1882, vol. XIV, no. 344.

Darton, N. H., W. S. Bayley, R. D. Salisbury, and H. B. Kummel. *Passiac Folio, New Jersey–New York.* Geologic Atlas of the United States, 1908, US Geological Survey, Folio 557.

DeCoste, P. E., and R. J. Dupont. 2009, *Hiking New Jersey: A Guide to 50 of the Garden State's Greatest Hiking Adventures*. Guilford, CT: Morris Book Publishing, 2009.

Drake, Avery A., and Jack B. Epstein. *The Martinsburg Formation (Middle and Upper Ordovician) in the Delaware Valley, Pennsylvania–New Jersey, Contributions to Stratigraphy*. Geological Survey Bulletin 1244-H, 1967, United States Geological Survey.

Drake, Avery A. Jr., Richard A. Volkert, Donald H. Monteverde, Gregory C. Herman, Hugh F. Houghton, Ronald A. Parker, and Richard F. Dalton. *Bedrock Geologic Map of Northern New Jersey*. US Geological Survey Miscellaneous Investigations, Map I-2540-A, 1996.

Dyson, James L. *Geology and Mineral Resources of the Southern Half of the New Bloomfield Quadrangle, Pennsylvania*. Atlas 137cd, Pennsylvania Geological Survey, 1967.

El-Ashry, M. T. *New Devonian Coral Reef from Monroe County, Eastern Pennsylvania*. Pennsylvania Academy of Science Proceedings, 1971, v. 45, pp. 5–8.

Ellison, R. L. *Stratigraphy and Paleontology of the Mahantango Formation in South-Central Pennsylvania*. General Geology Report 48, Pennsylvania Geological Survey, 1965.

Epstein, J. B., W. D. Sevon, and J. D. Glaeser. *Geology and mineral resources of the Lehighton and Palmerton quadrangles, Carbon and Northampton Counties, Pennsylvania*. Atlas 195cd, Pennsylvania Geological Survey, 1974.

Geyer, Alan R., and William H. Bolles. *Outstanding Scenic Geologic Features of Pennsylvania*. Environmental Geology Report 7, Pennsylvania Geologic Survey, 1979.

Geyer, Alan R., C. Gray, D. B. McLaughlin, and J. R. Moseley. *Geology of the Lebanon Quadrangle*. Atlas 167c, Pennsylvania Geologic Survey, 1958.

Geyer, Alan R., Robert C. Smith II, and J. H. Barnes. *Mineral Collecting in Pennsylvania*. General Geology Report 33, Pennsylvania Geologic Survey, 1976.

Gordon, Samuel P. *The Mineralogy of Pennsylvania*. Special Publication No. 1, Academy of Natural Sciences of Philadelphia, 1922.

Gunnarson, Robert. *The Story of the North Central Railway: From Baltimore to Lake Ontario*. Waukesha, WI: Kalmbach Publishing Company, 1991.

Haley, B. R., H. H. Arndt, H. E. Rothrock, and H. C. Wagner. *Geology of Anthracite in the western part of the Ashland Quadrangle, Pennsylvania.* US Geological Survey Coal Investigations Map C-13, 1953.

Harper, John. *Iron in Venango County: Oil's Older Sibling.* Pennsylvania Geology, vol. 30, no. 1/2, spring/summer 1999.

Harper, John A., and Loren E. Babcock. *Geotectonic Environment of the Lake Erie Crustal Block.* Sixty-third Annual Field Conference of Pennsylvania Geologists, 1998.

Henderson, William A. *Mullica Hill, New Jersey.* Mineralogical Record 11, 1980, pp. 307–11.

Hickok, W. O. IV, and F. T. Moyer. *Geology and Mineral Resources of Fayette County, Pennsylvania.* County Report 26, Pennsylvania Geological Survey, 1940.

Hoskins, D. M. *Geology and Mineral Resources of the Millersburg 15-minute Quadrangle, Dauphin, Juniata, Northumberland, Perry, and Snyder Counties, Pennsylvania.* Atlas 146, Pennsylvania Geologic Survey, 1976.

Hoskins, Donald M. *Fossil Collecting in Pennsylvania.* General Geology Report 40, Second Edition, Pennsylvania Geological Survey, 1969.

Hoskins, Donald M., Jon D. Inners, and John A. Harper. *Fossil Collecting in Pennsylvania.* General Geology Report 40, Third Edition, Pennsylvania Geological Survey, 1983.

Inners, J. D. *The Fossiliferous Stony Brook Beds (Upper Devonian) of Columbia County, Pennsylvania.* Pennsylvania Geology, 1981, vol. 12, no. 5, pp. 8–13.

————. *Spiral feeding-organ supports preserved in the brachiopod Athyris spiriferoides (Eaton), Rockville, Dauphin County, Pennsylvania.* Pennsylvania Geology, 1984, v. 15.

Janosov, Robert A. *Concrete City: Garden Village of the Anthracite Region.* Pennsylvania Heritage, 1987, #23, summer 1997, Pennsylvania Historical & Museum Commission.

Jengo, J. W. *Stratigraphic framework and sequence stratigraphy of sections of the Cretaceous age Raritan-Magothy Formations, Middlesex County, New Jersey.* Northeastern Geology and Environmental Science, 1995, vol. 17, pp. 223–46.

Lapham, Davis, M. *Leonhardite and Laumontite in Diabase from Dillsburg, Pennsylvania.* American Mineralogist, 1963, vol. 48, pp. 683–8.

Lapham, Davis M., and Alan R. Geyer. *Mineral Collecting in Pennsylvania: General Geology Report 33.* Third Edition, Pennsylvania Geological Survey, 1969.

Lapham, Davis M., and Carlyle Gray. *Geology and Origin of the Triassic Magnetite Deposit and Diabase at Cornwall, Pennsylvania.* Mineral Resources Report M56, Pennsylvania Geologic Survey, 1972.

Lenik, Edward J. *Iron Mine Trails: A history and hiker's guide to the historic iron mines of the New Jersey and New York Highlands.* Published 1996 by New York–New Jersey Trail Conference, G.P.O. Box 2250, New York, NY 10016.

MacLachlan, D. B. *Structure and stratigraphy of the limestones and dolomites of Dauphin County, Pennsylvania.* General Geology Report 44, Pennsylvania Geological Survey, 1967.

———. *Geology and mineral resources of the Reading and Birdsboro quadrangles, Berks County, Pennsylvania.* Atlas 187cd, Pennsylvania Geological Survey, 1992.

Manchester, James G. *The Minerals of the Bergen Archways.* American Mineralogist, 1919, vol. 4, pp. 219–29.

Meisler, Harold, and A. E. Becher. *Hydrogeology of the Carbonate Rocks of the Lancaster 15-Minute Quadrangle, Southeastern Pennsylvania.* Water Resources Report 26, Pennsylvania Geological Survey, 1979.

Miller, B. L., D. M. Fraser, R. L. Miller, and others [1941]. *Lehigh County, Pennsylvania.* Pennsylvania Geological Survey, 4th ser., County Report 39.

Nickelsen, R. P. *Sequence of structural stages of the Alleghany orogeny, Bear Valley strip mine, Shamokin, Pa.* American Journal of Science, vol. 279, pp. 225–71, 1979.

Owens, James P., and James P. Minard. *Pre-Quaternary Geology of the Bristol Quadrangle, NJ-PA.* GQ-342, United States Geological Survey, 1964.

Palache, C. *The Minerals of Franklin and Sterling Hill, Sussex County, New Jersey.* US Geological Survey Professional Paper (with map), 1935, 180, 135pp.

Peacor, D. R., and P. J. Dunn. *Petersite: A REE and Phosphate Analog of Mixite.* American Mineralogist, 1982, 67:1039–42.

Pennsylvania Geological Survey, 2000, *Physiographic Provinces of Pennsylvania, Map 13.*

Pennsylvania Geology, 1969, *Columnar Jointing in South Mountain*, vol. 1, no. 2.

Pennsylvania Geology, 1969, *Quartz Roses for Your Garden,* author unavailable, vol. 1, no. 4.

Peters, Joseph J. *Triassic Traprock Minerals of New Jersey.* Rocks and Minerals, vol. 59, no. 4, July/Aug. 1984.

Pierotti, G. M., R. Mathur, R. C. Smith II, and F. Barra. *Re-Os molybdenite ages for the Antietam Reservoir, eastern Pennsylvania, a story of open-system behavior Re-Os isotopes in molybdenite.* Geological Society of America, Abstracts with Programs, vol. 38, no. 2, p. 24, Northeastern Section. Forty-first Annual Meeting, March 20–22, 2006, Harrisburg, PA.

Puffer, J., and J. Peters. *Magnetite Veins in Diabase of Laurel Hill, New Jersey.* Economic Geology, 1974, vol. 69, pp. 1294–9.

Root, Samuel I. *Geology and Mineral Resources of the Harrisburg West Area, Cumberland and York Counties, Pennsylvania.* Atlas 148ab, Pennsylvania Geologic Survey, 1977.

Schwimmer, Reed A. *Two Exceptional Educational Field Sites in Northern New Jersey.* Geological Society of America, Abstracts with Programs, vol. 44, no. 2, p. 78, Northeastern Section. Forty-seventh Annual Meeting, March 18–20, 2012, Hartford, CT.

Shannon, Earl V. *The serpentine locality at Montville, New Jersey.* American Mineralogist, 1927, vol. 12, no. 2.

Sheppard, R. A., and R. E. Hunter. *Chamosite Oolites in the Devonian of Pennsylvania.* Journal of Sedimentary Petrology, 1960, vol. 30, pp. 585–8.

Simonsen, A. H. *Paleoecology of fenestrate bryozoans in the Wymps Gap Limestone of southwestern Pennsylvania.* Pennsylvania Geology, 1981, vol. 12, no. 2.

Smith, R.C., and B. J. O'Neill. *A New Triassic Copper Occurrence at Rossville, Pennsylvania.* Pennsylvania Geology, 1973, vol. 4, no. 1.

Smith, Robert C. II. *The Mineralogy of Pennsylvania, 1966–1975.* Special Publication No. 1, Friends of Mineralogy, 1978, Pennsylvania Chapter, Inc.

———. *New Molybdenite Occurrence in Berks County, Pennsylvania.* Pennsylvania Geology, 1975, vol. 6, no. 6, p. 16.

Stepanski, Scott, and Karenne Snow. *Gem Trails of Pennsylvania and New Jersey.* Baldwin Park, CA: Gem Guide Books Company, 2000.

Stephens, G. C., T. O. Wright, and L. B. Platt. *Geology of the Middle Ordovician Martinsburg Formation and Related Rocks in Pennsylvania.* Forty-seventh Annual Field Conference of Pennsylvania Geologists, 1982.

Stose, G. W., and A. I. Jonas. *Geology and Mineral Resources of York County, Pennsylvania.* County Report 67, Pennsylvania Geological Survey, 1939.

Stose, R. W. *Geology and Mineral Resources of Greene County, Pennsylvania.* County Report 30, Pennsylvania Geological Survey, 1932.

Swatara State Park, Lebanon and Schuylkill Counties. Park Guide 16, Pennsylvania Trail of Geology (no date available), Pennsylvania Geologic Survey.

Thomlinson, Harold W. *Idiomorphic Cordierite from Safe Harbor, Pennsylvania.* American Mineralogist, 1942, vol. 27, pp. 646–8.

Thompson, R. R. *Lithostratigraphy of the Middle Ordovician Salona and Coburn Formations in Central Pennsylvania.* General Geology Report 38, Pennsylvania Geological Survey, 1963.

Turley, M. R. *Upper Devonian Sediments of the Bedford Quadrangle.* M.S. thesis, Pennsylvania State University, 99 pp., scale 1:62,500, 1952.

Vassiliou, Andreas H. *Uranium and rare earth mineralization at the Bemco Mine near Cranberry Lake, New Jersey.* Field Studies of New Jersey Geology and Guide to Field Trips, Fifty-second Annual Meeting of the New York State Geological Association, Warren Manspeizer, ed., 1980.

Wood, C. R., and D. B. MacLachlan. *Geology and Groundwater Resources of Northern Berks County, Pennsylvania.* Pennsylvania Geological Survey, 1978, 4th ser., Water Resource Report 44.

Woodward, Herbert P. *Copper Mines and Mining in New Jersey.* Bulletin 57, Geologic Survey of New Jersey, 1944.

INDEX

ABOUT THE AUTHOR

Robert Beard is a geologist and has collected rocks for over 30 years. He received his B.A. in geology from California State University, Chico. He attended the University of New Mexico as a graduate student in geology and spent considerable time looking for rocks in New Mexico's mountains and deserts. He worked briefly for a mining company as part of an exploration team during his first summer in New Mexico, got to see many different types of mineral deposits and geologic terrains, and developed a good understanding of minerals and how to find them. He received his M.S. in geology from UNM at a time when the mining and oil industries were flat on their backs, but the environmental cleanup industry was just getting started. He moved to Harrisburg, Pennsylvania, to pursue a career as an environmental geologist. Since then he has remained alert for opportunities to see geology and collect rocks, minerals, and fossils, as he was taught that the best geologist is the one that has seen the most rocks. He has collected rocks throughout most regions of the United States, Europe, and the Caribbean, and the past few years he has focused on finding new collecting sites in Pennsylvania and New Jersey. He is a contributing editor to *Rock & Gem* magazine and has written for *Rock & Gem* since 1993. He currently lives in Harrisburg with his wife, Rosalina, and his two children, Daniel and Roberta.